Strengths Oriented Selection

Strategies for Attracting
and
Assessing Great Talent

A SUCCESSPATH SERIES BOOK

DALE COBB

Published by Career Media, a division of SUCCESSPATH Career Development, Inc.

Career Media books may be purchased in bulk for educational, business, fundraising, or sales promotional use.

Library of Congress Cataloging-in-Publication Data

Cobb, Dale, 1957-
  Strengths Oriented Selection – Strategies for Attracting and Assessing Great Talent/Dale Cobb

ISBN-13: 9781792980541

DEDICATION

Thank you to my parents,
Allen and Frances Cobb
who always encouraged me
to pursue my dreams…

And to my beautiful wife and editor
Susy who stood by me when
that wasn't going so well.

CONTENTS

Read This First!

The purpose of this report is to help you rock staffing! The success of your business largely depends on your ability to attract, hire, position, re-position, promote and retain top talent. It's written especially for start up business owners and those in the small and medium size business phase.

Startups rarely give enough attention to hiring the first few people, but as Steve Jobs said, "When you're in a start-up, **the first ten people will determine whether the company succeeds or not.** Each is 10 percent of the company. So why wouldn't you take as much time as necessary to find all the A players? If three were not so great, why would you want a company where 30 percent of your people are not so great? A small company depends on great people much more than a big company does."

Excellence in Business author Tom Peters echoes, "We are concerned about hiring, no doubt about it. But do we treat it strategically as the most important aspect of business whether you're a 4 person body shop or *Siemans*? Are we professional students of hiring? Effective hiring = A craft, a profession with a body of knowledge to be mastered."

And *Google* Director of Leadership and Development says, "Development can help great people become even better – but if I had a dollar to spend, I'd spend… 70 cents… getting the right person in the door."

This book is about Strengths Oriented Sourcing and Selection then moves into Strengths Oriented Development and offers some positive direction on what to do if you make hiring errors.

The report is based on my experience…

Four Decades In The Work Place In Some Very Different Contexts…

1970s Family Construction Business

1980s Self Employed Specialty Contractor

1990s Sales Representative National Company

      Sales Representative for Staffing Company

2000s Manager/Trainer National Company

Served On Boards of Three Non-Profits

10 Years Working Candidates in Career Transition

15 Years of Research on the Staffing Process

Strengths Oriented Staffing forms the S.O.S. acrostic or acronym. SOS is a universal symbol of "HELP". As we will see in later sections, Strengths Oriented Staffing is designed to help organizations, employees and candidates… even those that are not hired in profound ways.

You Have A Strategy

You have a staffing strategy that is perfectly designed to get the results you're getting!

This book is filled with Strengths Oriented Staffing Strategies.

Universal Strategies – There are universal staffing strategies. You will have some kind of job description even if it's not formalized or well-crafted. You'll probably use some form of advertising, even if it's word of mouth. You'll have some form of interview process and so-forth.

Cultural Strategies – You are part of a distinct culture. Some of your strategies will come from that culture. If you're reading this in the United States or United Kingdom there will be nuances that relate back to that culture.

Regional Strategies – In the United States, you may do some things because you live in the South, the Northeast, or the West. Some of this may have to do with regional nuances and some of it may even have to do with individual state laws. Some may have to do with whether or not your business is in a rural, suburban or urban setting.

Individual Principles – There are staffing strategies you will incorporate because you have a unique success style. Some strategies will work for you and not for others and vice versa.

Seasonal Principles – You may need to hire differently in the summer or around Christmas. You may get in a pinch and need temporary help.

Situational Principles – Every hiring situation is unique. To be legal you must have a rigorous standard that doesn't discriminate… and still remain flexible.

Strengths Principles – From beginning-to-end, the Strengths Oriented Approach to staffing is about hiring candidates only for roles that involve topics they're passionate about and the talents they're talented to perform. A strengths orientation reforms the entire hiring process. It starts with help writing a strengths based job description, a strengths based advertisement or job posting, a strengths based application, and then conducting a strengths based interview.

I've done extensive research on companies like:

Facebook

Apple

Google

Cisco

Standard Charter Bank

Jancoa Janitorial – Mary & Tony Miller

Some of the research comes from successful business leaders including:

Tony Robbins

Richard Branson

Warren Buffett

Bill Gates

Steve Jobs

Other research comes from the strengths based materials and workshops of:

Gallup

The Marcus Buckingham Company

Harrison Assessments

Strengthsmatch - Sally Bibb

Harvard University – Dr. Timothy Butler

O*NET – Occupational Information Network – Department of Labor

Handbook of Human Abilities – Edwin A. Fleishman and Maureen Reilly

...Books like:

Getting The People Equation Right by Logan Loomis

Smart & Gets Things Done by Joel Spolsky

How Google Works by Eric Schmidt & Jonathan Rosenberg

Work Rules! That Will Transform How You Lead by Lazlo Bock

Principles by Ray Dalio

And finally:

I've had thirty years of experience hiring in entrepreneurial start-ups, corporate environments and non-profits. I also led countless interview debriefs of candidates just returning from job interviews. As a career advisor I asked detailed questions of each applicant. I often got great ideas and many insights on the creative methods small businesses were using to identify applicant strengths.

"Talent – Hiring is the most important thing you do."

~Eric Schmidt, Executive Chairman, *Google*

Introduction

I grew up working in a family construction business. Dad was always hiring people. In his later years he owned the local *Spherion Personnel* franchise and hired thousands of workers. I saw the hiring successes and the failures.

In my late teen years I caught the entrepreneurial bug and began hiring workers myself. Later, I worked as the West Coast hiring manager for a large national company. For eight years I interviewed candidates from San Diego to Seattle. I really enjoyed the process of trying to match up the various strengths of different candidates for the roles I was asked to fill.

Eventually I began to understand my earlier quote from Excellence in Business expert Tom Peters, "Effective hiring = A craft, a profession with a body of knowledge to be mastered."

Most of the hiring in America is done at small businesses by owners who don't take the time to think through what it takes to hire great people. But all the best businesses do. This is an unqualified statement without exception. All excellent businesses hire terrific people and it doesn't happen by accident.

In his wonderful book, *Good to Great*, Jim Collins says that all great businesses first get the right people on the bus and then get them in the right seats. And I would add, they adjust those seats to fit the employee. They resist changing the employee. They change the job. Mediocre to good companies often get the right people on the bus... and then screw it up. They hire great people and then go to work trying to "fix" them. They rarely get them in the right seats. The attitude of many employers and hiring managers is, "That's the job, take it or leave it."

Strengths Oriented Staffing

The key issue of selection and hiring is always contribution and added value. Will the candidate help solve a problem that needs solving or help reach a goal that needs to be reached? Will they pull on the right end of the rope? Will they represent and build your reputation or brand? And strengths are how they do that. I define a strength as any resource, internal or external that makes a contribution and adds value to an organization. I believe all candidates should be viewed in light of eight considerations.

7 Elements of Strengths Based Selection

I believe all great staffing is optimally viewed through the lens of eight specific components. To introduce these elements, let me offer a very brief explanation and then a personal example from my own life. In later chapters I'll do a deeper dive with each component.

The first element is **Passion!** This should be the most important consideration when pulling someone on your team. This means you hire them for workplace topics and tasks for which they have a natural interest. Usually, when I talk about passion, I mean the topic, career area, some type of solution, outcome or result. I have a passion for helping individuals and organizations increase their success. I've been fascinated by this since I was 14 years old. I've studied athletes, businesses, coaches, comedians, doctors, educators, film makers, ministers, military and political leaders and sales people. I have a passion to understand what makes individuals and organizations successful.

The second component of great hiring is **Talent**. These are the inclinations and instincts people are born with. Your unique mix of talents make some tasks seem almost effortless and enjoyable and your lack of talent will make other tasks seem extraordinarily difficult and sometimes even miserable. Talents, as we will see later, can be thought about as aptitudes, activities and approaches. In my case, I have a talent for in-depth research and writing in a conversational style that organizes mountains of material into memorable chunks that others can relate, assimilate and apply to their life.

The third element of a strong hiring process is **Personality**. I'm not talking about a good personality or a bad personality. I'm talking about a personality that is a good match for the work performed. Everyone has a temperament, traits and characteristics that make them a good fit for one job and a poor fit for another. I'm moderately introverted, meaning I can work for long stretches without a lot of human interaction. In short bursts I enjoy jumping the line into extroversion for coaching and training sessions.

The fourth component is personal **Values**. These are the ideals, priorities and motivations that often make a candidate a great fit for one company or organization and a poor fit for another. Values are drivers and motivators that will move you to select a certain church, a political party and sometimes even what region, state or country you decide to live in. My highest workplace values are Discovery, Autonomy, Variety and Excellence.

The fifth area we consider is **Knowledge**. Does the candidate have the vocabulary, understand key principles, concepts and rules? Knowledge is often collapsed together with skills and that's a mistake. They are two different pieces of the puzzle. My learning library consists of several thousand resources including books, audio, DVD and other digital components.

The sixth aspect are **Skills** that match job requirements. This is often the only component many organizations and hiring managers look at or consider. Skill is a critical piece of whether or not a person can do the job.

3

consider. Skill is a critical piece of whether or not a person can do the job. But it's not the only piece and this is why most companies make poor hiring decisions. It doesn't give you any clue as to how much a candidate wants to do the tasks and activities. As a stand alone, the candidates' skill set offers no clue as to how fast a candidate will learn similar or related tasks. My skills include compiling, reading, interviewing, keyboarding and blogging.

The seventh component of great hiring is **Character**. Will the candidate consistently show up for work? Will they show up on time? Will they show up clean and sober? Are they trustworthy?

Other Strengths Based Elements

There are several other strengths based elements worth considering as well. These include things like project phase preferences, geographical proximity, tools, transportation and even chronotype.

Competencies... Meh!

A competency is the ability to do a job. It doesn't necessarily suggest how well the job is done, how fast it is done or how much the individual with the competency wants to do the job. Honestly, I loathe the word and humbly request that you drop it from your vocabulary. Competency is a tepid luke-warm word that suggests mediocrity or average. If that's what you want to hire, hold on to the word.

Strengths Oriented Staffing is about hiring people who are insanely great at what they do. It's about hiring people who are extremely internally motivated and highly gifted for the tasks you are hiring them to do. Competent would be a very poor way to describe them.

Dream Jobs and Dream Employees

People of all ages, but especially young people and students are counseled directly and indirectly, not to get their hopes up. They are told that work is supposed to be hard. "There are no perfect jobs," they are cautioned.

Employers are similarly warned, "There are no perfect candidates." Perfect may not be the word I would use for a job or a candidate. But there are awesome fits, average fits and awful fits. Candidates who don't understand this at a deep level will consistently end up failing at work they hate. Companies who don't embrace this at a deep level will consistently end up with employees who fail at work they hate.

The Strengths Oriented Staffing Process – The "A" Game Method

In this book you will get a chance to consider Strengths Oriented Staffing principles as they relate to:

Attributes – All work roles have attributes – that is characteristics, features and traits. All candidates have attributes – characteristics, features and traits. The secret is to get them matched up with increasing precision. Strengths Oriented Staffing begins with a better understanding of the job and moves on to gain a better understanding of the type of person who will excel in the role.

Accurate Job Descriptions – A job description should focus on the key results a candidate will be required to produce and the key attributes that will ensure they can do that… and just as important, want to do it. Traditional Competency Oriented Descriptions usually focus on education, experience, knowledge and skills. Strengths Oriented Descriptions incorporate those factors, and add a strong emphasis on job related Passion or Deeply Imbedded Life Interests combined with relevant Aptitudes, Activities and Approaches that relate to their talent.

Advertisements – A terrific job advertisement should attract great applicants and repel unqualified ones. Traditional advertisements focus on a few elements of the job itself. Strengths Oriented Advertisements are applicant focused, describing key traits of a perfect candidate. Strengths Oriented ads should generate a strong response in the reader – YES! THAT'S ME! or NO! THAT's NOT ME AT ALL!

Applications – A great job application should be fun and worthy of a little positive gossip. Traditional job applications are extremely predictable, boring, difficult to fill out and do little to help an applicant decide if the job is a good fit. Strengths Oriented Applications encourage self discovery. They help a candidate understand the best version of themselves, including their intrinsic passion, natural talents, personality traits and values.

Assessment – The best candidate assessments, like the Strengths Oriented Application are fun and create a desire for the applicant to rush out and tell all their friends! It may include a psychometric indicator, a work sample and interview questions that are enjoyable to answer. The outcome should always be that both the candidate and the company have received great insight on the job fit.

Appointments – The selection process should leave both the candidate and the company with a clear understanding of hiring decision. Ideally, the applicants that weren't hired would be encouraged how to reapply for positions that are a better fit. In cases where the decision making process was close or a virtual tie, the applicant would be encouraged to stay in touch for the next opening.

Assimilation – Strengths Oriented Onboarding focuses on delivering critical information and training in a way that corresponds to the new associates Learning Style. Does the new associate learn best by watching, reading, listening, experimenting, writing? How can you tweak your training to accommodate that style?

Appraisal – In order to advance, associates need feedback – information on the results they've achieved and feed forward – information on ways to get better. The traditional performance appraisal focuses on weaknesses and how to improve. The Strengths Oriented Appraisal focuses on success and strengths and how to expand and build on these positives.

Alignment – Weekly alignment meetings are a critical component of Strengths Oriented Staffing. These brief one-to-one meetings are designed to insure that the attributes of the work role continue to match the strengths of the associate.

Anchors - Jobs tend to creep. A candidate is hired to do one kind of work and the job description begins to shift each week. For example, the new employee is hired to meet with customers and then a new reporting system is implemented taking several additional hours to complete. Anchoring also means avoiding the *Peter Principle* – Promoting an associate into an area they have less affinity and aptitude for.

Advancement – Strengths Oriented Career Development is built on the idea of amplifying an associates strengths and helping them work around their weaknesses. An assessment like Strengthsfinder is a wonderful starting point to help an employee better understand the unique ways they approach their work.

Attrition – What is your retention and turnover? Are you losing great people? In this section we look at strategies designed to turn your non-stick *Teflon* company into a full-fledge *Velcro* company!

I work both sides of the aisle, but this book is specifically for those who are responsible for selection and hiring. I urge you to take complete responsibility for hiring candidates who are an awesome fit for the job and insuring they stay in roles where they will excel. This will require passion on your part, some talent, as well as acquired skills and knowledge. If you don't have the passion and talent for hiring great people, stop doing it. You are ruining your organization and you yourself are a terrible example for everyone around you. You are ruining the lives of the candidates you select. Find other work… please.

If you do have a passion for this work, make it your mission to help everyone you interview connect with their dream job, the one that fits them perfectly. Part of my dream is to convince businesses of their moral responsibility to hire only those who are great fits for work that needs doing. Moral responsibility is strong language I know.

Human resource and hiring managers alike would be much better at their work if they began to view themselves more as vocational counselors who are working on behalf of both the candidate and the company. Stop trying to find someone who can do the job. Start looking for people who can't wait to do the tasks and activities within the job. **Become the dancing instructor who helps people tap dance to work every morning.** This added value service on your part will make your company one of the most sought after employers in the world.

"Whichever way you care to slice the data, the organization whose employees feel that their strengths are used every day is more powerful and more robust."

~Marcus Buckingham

Chapter One
One Question That Predicts Performance

What's the difference between the great teams and the not so great teams inside a company? *Gallup* has discovered that there is one question… One question which predicts most effectively, most consistently whether an employee will be an awesome performer, an average performer or an awful performer. The question is deceptively simple, "**At work do you have the opportunity to do what you do best every day?**" "At work do you have the opportunity to use your strengths every day?" The teams where the associates say that they do have that opportunity, consistently and massively outperform the teams where employees answer in the negative.

In 1975 only 200 books were published on managing and leading. By 1997, more than 600 books were available. Between 1975 and 1997 business authors have offered up over 9000 different systems, principles, and ideas to explain management and leadership. Much of the advice is conflicting, impressionistic, and anecdotal… just a bunch of stories.

By contrast, the *Gallup Organization* has studied great companies, great teams and great individual performances with a detail orientation bordering on obsessive. For over 50 years they have surveyed over 10 million employees. One survey alone included 198,000 associates working in 7,939 business units within 36 companies.

As of 2001, *Gallup* had a total database around the above workplace question. It included responses from 1.7 million employees, from 101 companies in 63 countries. They have conducted over 20,000 interviews with senior leaders and studied more than one million work teams.

They interviewed over 80,000 managers in over 400 companies. Each manager was interviewed for 1.5 hours using open-ended questions. The answers were tape recorded, read and re-read by social scientists. The accumulated audio included over 120,000 hours of recordings and produced five million pages of transcript. The scientists compared answers of high performing managers and average managers. They looked for patterns. All of this was done within a wide variety of industries including with hotel supervisors, sales managers, manufacturing team leaders, professional sports coaches, pub managers, public school superintendents, captains, majors, and colonels in the military, and even deacons, priests, and pastors.

One Glaring Pattern

When you go into organizations and study them closely, you make one discovery and you make that discovery every time. You find out that there is a huge range of performance - team by team within the same company.

The positive answer to one question predicts performance most reliably…

"At work, do you have the opportunity to do what you do best everyday?"

According to *Gallup* that one question reliably predicts:

Odds you will work on a high performing team – 5x greater
Customer metrics – 12% Higher
Productivity – 18% Higher
Profitability – 16 % Higher
Absenteeism – 37% Lower
Turnover (High Turnover Organizations) – 25% Lower
Turnover (Low Turnover Organizations) – 49% Lower

Theft – 27% Lower
Safety Incidents – 41% Lower
Quality Defects – 60% Lower

It's great if you can adopt strengths based recruiting approaches early in the life of the company, but transitions to this approach can show fast results. In Sally Bibbs book, *Strengths Based Recruitment & Development,* she offers several examples of organizations making the shift, particularly in the United Kingdom. *Standard Chartered Bank* introduced Strengths Based techniques in 2000… They introduced Strengths Based Recruitment for sales roles. The results were impressive. Between three and six months after starting in the job, employees hired using the Strengths Based Recruiting approach were on average bringing in 40% more revenue than those hired using the previous approach.

Lisa Robbins, the HR director for *Starbucks* in the United Kingdom, reported in a 2014 interview with *HR Magazine*, "Staff turnover among our new apprentices has reduced by a third and we anticipate that by applying these recruitment strategies, we can continue to reduce this rate and retain future leaders in our business… A significant benefit of this process is not relying on a potential employee's work experience at the interview stage – the strengths and motivator profile allows candidates to share more examples from their life experience, which is very relevant for our apprentice candidates who are usually coming to us straight out of school or college."

"If you hire people whose passion intersects with the job, they won't require any supervision at all. They will manage themselves better than anyone could ever manage them. Their fire comes from within, not from without."

~Stephen Covey

Chapter Two
Staffing for Passion

19th Century writer and philosopher Henry David Thoreau wrote, "Do not hire a man who does your work for money, but him who does it for love of it." Financial guru Dave Ramsey is even more straight forward, "One of the rules when coming on board at the *Dave Ramsey Company* is that you have to love your job. I will fire you just for hating your job." Ramsey continues, "Passion Matters. When we're focused on and operating in our strengths and passions, nothing can hold us back…. When you love what you do you will work like crazy – but it will never feel like work."

The first element of *Strengths Oriented Selection* is **PASSION**. Synonyms for passion are natural affinity, appetite, gusto, avidity, eagerness, fascination, intense interest, relish, delight, fun, enthusiasm, excitement, energy, ambition, desire or simply, what you love. Passion is a topic or task that draws a worker in. It's an activity or subject area that makes them feel strong.

Harvard University career services director, Dr. Timothy Butler refers to passion as, "Deeply Embedded Life Interests". Butler writes, "Think of a deeply embedded life interest as a geothermal pool of superheated water. It will rise to the surface in one place as a hot spring and in another as a geyser. But beneath the surface—at the core of the individual—the pool is constantly bubbling. Deeply embedded life interests always seem to find

15

expression, even if a person has to change jobs—or careers—for that to happen. Mature adults have particular patterns of lifelong passions that remain stable over long periods."

Facebook Chief Operating Officer Sheryl Sandberg says, "You will not be as successful as you could be if you only like what you do and don't love it." Always hire the candidate with the most passion and interest for the type of work you need done. This is especially true when two candidates are equally experienced, equally credentialed, and equally capable. But often you would be much better off hiring the candidate who lacks the credentials or experience, but has the passion. Search for the candidate with a passion for the business, a zeal for the industry, an excitement, a zest for the art and the craft of what makes a company in your industry succeed. Great companies have discovered that somebody who is passionate about the topics and tasks of the work grows faster and quickly passes the credentialed one.

Passionate people are inherently motivated, and driven to succeed, they try harder to find answers. They think up creative stuff on their own. They enjoy the business and are always thinking about it. They're always discovering new things and figuring out additional ways that the business could succeed.

Passionate people care more than the average employee, they care more than the average applicant, and they care more than you. If you want to hire employees who will succeed in their work, you need to hire them to do what they're actually passionate about. Otherwise, you're really helping any organization that competes with you.

The *Dictionary of Occupational Titles* lists over 13,000 potential occupations. Each of these represent a possible combination of subject areas and work activities. Here is a much briefer list to help you think about possibilities and passions. Put a list like this in front of the candidates you are considering for hire. Ask them which of the topics and tasks they are passionate about.

Government, Law and Protection
Law, Court, Legislation, Labor Relations, Executive, Foreign Policy, Politics, Military, Fire Fighting, Police, Security, Investigation, Secret Service, Criminology

Arts & Entertainment, Culture and Sports
Architecture, Paintings, Photographs, Fashion, Interiors, Design, Sculpture, Flowers, Dance, Music, Theater, Collections, Sports, Music, Festivals, Animation,

Media
Language, Writing, Editing, Producing, Speaking, Literature, Journalism, Library, Television, Film, Social Media, Broadcasting, Creative Director, Art Director, Copywriter, Advertising, Digital Media, Graphics, Animation, Reporter

Education
Teaching, Adult Education, University, Junior College, Vocation, Early Childhood, Elementary, High School, Middle School, Corporate Training, Human Potential, Literacy, GED, Career Services, Counseling, Coaching, Advising, Mentoring

Science & Technology - Computing and Electronics
Biology, Physics, Engineering, Networking, Programing, Software, Hardware, Developing, Internet, Gaming, Social Network, Data Base, Cell Phones, Computers, Television, Cameras, Music Players, Appliances, Ag Science, Medicine, Pharmaceuticals, Dental, Nursing, Laboratories, Radiology, Emergency, Fitness, Physical Therapy, Neurology

Business
Administration, Entrepreneurship, Marketing, Sales, Operations, Production, Retail, Real Estate, Restaurants, Advertising, Insurance, Manufacturing, Operations, Customer Service, Distribution, Transportation, Warehousing, Hospitality, Statistics, Economics, Records, Accounting, Finance, Banking, Investments, Construction

Family
Marriage/Family, Parenting, Food, Cleaning, Child Care, Clothing, Shopping, Budgets, Decoration, Home Schooling, Nutrition, Child Development, Tailoring, Sewing, Mr. Mom

Faith
Ministries, Children, Youth, Hospitality, Small Groups, Bible Study, Evangelism, Serving, Spiritual Gifts, Church Plants, Missions, Teaching, Preaching, Counseling, Recovery, Social Work, Rehabilitation, Marriage/Family, Hunger, Children, Substance Abuse, Housing/Shelter, Elderly

Active Image Gathering

The point of Image Gathering is not to have a candidate choose a profession or career from the list. What you want an applicant to do is select from the list and then describe the specific topical engagement task activity they see themselves enjoying. When I was 5 years old I wanted to be a cowboy like Roy Rogers. I had no idea that being a cowboy meant cold lonely nights miles away from the nearest *Starbucks*. I thought cowboys chased bad guys. Today I know this meant that I wanted a career that helped people. And I wanted to do something that was even a bit heroic.

That's the kind of information you would want to gather from a candidate. Is there a connection between these images and the actual work they would be performing?

Ask them, did any of these topics stir something inside as you read them? What images came to mind? What work did you actually see yourself performing? Ask them to describe it in some detail. Drill deeper… Have them write a job description that includes 20 tasks they see themselves performing in their ideal job. Ask follow up questions. **Did their eyes light up? Did they start talking faster? Did they get more animated?** Ask a candidate about their dream job. Have them pick one from the list. Does it have anything to do with what they are applying for? Are they really wanting another job and see this one as a stepping stone? Is the role you're offering just something to put a little money in their pocket and to get them by? If so, this isn't a good hiring strategy.

Did any of the topics or tasks make them want to vigorously pump their fist and yell, "YES"?

Embedded in the word "Y.E.S.", we can find other clues.

Yearning – Ask the candidate how they feel **before** engaging a specific topic or task? For which topics and tasks do they yearn, even crave involvement? Which ones do they long for?

Engaged – How do they feel **during** the engagement with this topic or task? Do they easily focus on it? Does it draw them in and then keep them there? Does time seem to fly by? Do they enjoy it? Does it energize them?

Mihaly Csikszentmihalyi (Chick-sent-me-high-ee) is a Hungarian immigrant and psychology professor who has spent much of his career investigating what he calls "Flow". **Flow is complete absorption.** In athletics, this flow state is often called "being in the zone". Jazz musicians refer to it as being "in the groove". It is a state of optimal productivity where an individual is fully immersed in what they are doing. In this state, a worker may lose all track of time.

Satisfaction - How do they feel **after** engagement with the topic or task? Some topics and tasks leave a worker fulfilled afterward. They leave them with a warm afterglow. And then that fulfillment and satisfaction should lead back to the **Y**earning where they started. When that happens, a victorious cycle has been built.

Don't Get Me Started!

Google uses the phrase "Don't Get Me Started" to describe someone who is talking about their passion. At *Google* interviews, they try to get a candidate started… started talking about the things that they are really excited about and enjoy doing. Do those things connect with the job? If so, you've got a strong candidate in front of you! Get them started.

Apple and Steve Jobs were famous for making passion the cornerstone of their hiring philosophy. Andy Hertzfeld, one of *Apple's* early software people describes the *Macintosh* hiring process, "After hours-long interviews, interviewees were shown the *Macintosh* prototypes. If they didn't respond with much enthusiasm, they didn't get the job. But if their eyes lit up, we knew they were one of us."

After a season of hiring experienced "professionals", Jobs gave up on that idea. He switched gears and began looking for people who were insanely great, with a passion for what they did. One example of *Apple's* passion-based hiring philosophy was bringing on Debi Coleman, a young 32-year-old *Stanford* Lit major. Coleman was brought in to run manufacturing despite having no prior experience in the field.

I heard Oprah Winfrey share this insight, "Every single person who is super successful always says in some form that following their bliss or **following their passion is the way to be the most successful** and empowered person." Isn't that what you want for every single person you hire? Don't you want that for everyone on your team?

I challenge you to make every part of your staffing process an event that will help a candidate get in touch with their passion and find work that connects with it.

In her booklet, *What I Know For Sure*, Oprah writes, "Have the **courage** to follow your passion. If you don't know what your passion is, realize that one reason for your existence on earth is to find it. **Your life's work is to find your life's work and then exercise the discipline, tenacity and hard work it takes to pursue it**. Ignoring your passion is like dying a slow death. Your life is speaking to you every day, all the time and your job is to listen and find the clues. Passion whispers to you through your feelings, beckoning you toward your highest good. **Pay attention to what makes you feel energized, connected, stimulated - what gives you your juice**. Do what you love, **give it back in the form of service**, and you will do more than succeed. You will triumph."

Napoleon Hill said, "No one is richer than the person who has found their labor of love and is busily engaged in performing it."

What if you began to see your work in sourcing, selection and hiring as nudging and encouraging candidates toward their passion? Not only will you hire the best people, you will become the most attractive place to work.

Hire "Batteries Included" People

Strategic Coach founder Dan Sullivan works with entrepreneurs around a concept he calls, "Batteries Included". Dan divides the whole human race into BNI (Batteries Not Included) and BI (Batteries Included). Did you ever buy a battery operated Christmas present? The person receiving the gift opened it up, but the batteries were not included. Often it is stamped right on the box - "Batteries Not Included". On the other hand, it is always so much more exciting when the gift works immediately because the batteries are included. The manufacturer is being very thoughtful and they want to make the experience a really pleasant one.

People are like that. There are people who are Batteries Not Included. They don't produce any energy for themselves. Then there are other people that come with their own batteries. They bring their own energy.

In talking about the concept, Michael Hyatt says, "I am willing to help people without batteries, but I am not willing to hire them. I want everyone in my organization to have their own battery pack. If they don't, they just deplete everyone else. I want my people working to grow my business and reach their potential—not wasting energy making up for someone's character deficit."

Help Candidates Find Their Mash Up

Road Trip Nation co-creator Nathan Gebhard talks about combining interests and passions. When doing high school presentations, he asks the students in the audience what they are interested in. He asks them to combine interests like art and writing, sports and science and then come up with an occupation. At one presentation, a student said, "I like walking and turtles. I want to be a turtle walker." So as part of the presentation, Nathan played a video, and behind the scenes had the staff "Google" "Turtle Walking." They literally found a woman who worked at a rehabilitation center for turtles. Within minutes they had the student up on stage, on the phone talking to a real-life turtle walker.

Growing up in the 1950s, Ed had two boyhood idols, Walt Disney and Albert Einstein. As he explains it, "Disney was all about inventing the new and Einstein was about explaining that which already was." Ed decided he wanted to be a *Disney* animator and pursued it. But it became clear his drawing wasn't good enough and the pathway to get there wasn't very well laid out. Ed decided to pursue his other love, science. He graduated with two degrees, one in physics and the other in a then emerging field called computer science.

Ed met a man who encouraged him to pursue an even more obscure subset of computer science. It was called computer graphics. All of a sudden, the other childhood dream was back in play. At age 26, Ed set a goal to develop a way to animate, not with pencil and paper, but using a computer. In 1972, he made his first short animated film. In 1986, he became the president of a new hardware company called *Pixar Image Computer*. Ed Catmull went on to co-found *Pixar Animation* collaborating with people like Steve Jobs and John Lassiter.

Hiring Passion ≠ Hiring Attitude

Hiring for passion is <u>NOT</u> the same thing as hiring for attitude or enthusiasm. Several decades ago, leaders in the Success Movement were trying to teach people that passion or enthusiasm could be conjured up. In my *Dale Carnegie Training*, we chanted, "To Be Enthusiastic, I Will Act Enthusiastic!" *Success Motivation Institute* founder, Paul J. Meyer taught us that we could increase our enthusiasm on a subject by studying it. The more we learned, the more enthusiasm we would generate. Both of these ideas have a measure of truth, but that's not what I'm talking about.

Consider what Jim Collins said in *Good to Great*, "**You can't manufacture passion or motivate people to feel passionate. You can only discover what ignites your passion** and the passions of those around you.."

Amazon founder Jeff Bezos agrees, "**One of the huge mistakes people make is that they try to force an interest on themselves. You don't choose your passions; your passions choose you.**"

That Kid Was A Find – The Staples Price Guy

In 1998, the *Cliff Freeman Agency* created an advertisement for *Staples* that I just loved. The 30 second spot featured an unnamed *Staples* store manager who was frustrated because he was constantly faced with store price reductions and the resulting package price sticker changes. He was frustrated until he "found" Willis, a young man who lived his passion making these changes. You may still be able to find the ad here: **http://www.tvspots.tv/video/8862/staples--price-guy**. The ad closes with Willis displaying over-the-top excitement for the new price change project.

The manager walks away with the final line, "That kid was a find."

This is a great example of what I'm talking about because it actually demonstrates both the passion for a particular kind of work and… the expressed enthusiasm. Passion and enthusiasm are related concepts as I describe them, but it's the underlying passion that you are looking for to make the best hire.

High Passion – Poor Attitude

Mark was a work associate that I grew to love over the years. He was truly passionate about his work. Mark was consistently a top 5 producer on a sales force of about 150 reps. He was also one of the smartest people I've ever met and took care of his customers with impeccable integrity. What makes Mark such an interesting case was that many of his managers hated him and upper management considered him a pain in backside. He was a consistent top performer, took great care of his customers and yet from management's standpoint, his attitude was terrible.

From my perspective, most of the problem was with management and not Mark. I often said, " If Mark were my rep I would personally wash his car every week." He was that valuable. Mark's attitude "problem" was that he believed his work associates should take their jobs as seriously as he took his. He had a low tolerance for associates who didn't take as good of care of his customers as he did. Mark was high passion and yet consistently carried a bit of a negative attitude. In my view, both the passion and the negative attitude actually served to make the company better.

I've never been a fan of the phrase, "Hire for attitude – Train for Skill." It has its place, but it's too simplistic. There are legitimate reasons to be concerned and sometimes that concern needs to be expressed forcefully. There is such a thing as "righteous anger". On the other hand, you want to build a "culture of honor", a place where every individual is respected, customers and associates alike. "Hire for Attitude – Train for Skill" also fails to acknowledge the role of natural talent, a subject I'll pick up in the next chapter.

Passion = Deeply Embedded Life Interest

Earlier in this chapter I offered Timothy Butler's phrase, *Deeply Embedded Life Interest* as a phrase that explains passion. He also uses the phrases, *Deep Interest Pattern* and *Deep Structure Interests*. Butler offers more on this topic, "Each of us has a unique pattern of interests, a 'potential self' that seeks expression. One of the most interesting findings in career psychology research is that underlying patterns of work interest are a relatively enduring feature of a person."

Butler continues, "There is evidence that, amid this stability, new experiences in work environments continue to influence the development of interests, but *within the contours of the deep interest pattern*. Deep structure interests are one of the most basic features of an individual. They are deeply rooted and enduring, and they naturally push to find an avenue of expression."

Butler offers up the artist Andy Warhol as an example. Warhol's *Deep Structure Interests* were realized through his work in advertising, paintings and films. Similarly Richard Feynman's deep structure interest is seen in his scientific research, his writings and his lectures. Butler contends that any work that is not adequately grounded in a person's *Deep Structure Interests* will not last. Albert Einstein might have become a mathematician or a chemist instead of a physicist, but he would never have made it as a military officer. Bill Gates would never have succeeded as a food services manager. This is not because either Einstein or Gates had a poor attitude.

Hiring people for the right positions begins with a search for each candidate's *Deep Structure Interest Patterns* and seeing if there is a match with an opening you have available.

Hiring people to work in their passion does not mean that success won't be hard for them. Steve Jobs told us that it is exactly because success is so very hard that we need to discover our passion.

Hiring someone to work in their passion does not put them on the pathway to an easy life. Passion Test author Janet Attwood addresses this, "Sometimes it's painful… Many people think that just because you live a passionate life you'll have no challenges, that once you know your passions it's like a smooth road, but it's not so. There are obstacles, there are challenges, there are moments when you go, 'I don't know whether to go right or left'."

Historically, passion incorporated the idea of sacrifice and suffering. I recommend watching *The Passion of the Christ* movie for the ultimate example of what I'm talking about. What is it that the potential employee loves so much that they are willing to sacrifice and suffer for it? What topics will they arrive early and stay late for? What tasks will so engage them that they forget about lunch?

But in his book, *Organizing Genius*, Warren Bennis brings this subject back around. He says, "Great Groups allow participants to find their workplace bliss." Bennis cites former *Xerox* executive Bob Sparicino as a negative example. Sparicino was known to say, "People shouldn't work because they love it. They should work because it hurts." Bennis concludes, "Talented people working because it hurts is a formula for organization disaster."

Talking to candidates about their intense interests and passion will set you apart from other employers in a very positive way. You will better communicate your interest in them personally and set the standard that you expect them to enjoy their job, even have fun at work.

More Thoughts on Passion

"Hire people who are super enthusiastic, self motivated and passionate. Don't hire people who just want a job. You will not be as successful as you could be if you only like what you do and don't love it."
~Eric Schmidt, Executive Chairman, *Google*

"Successful leaders of the future will have to tap into the tremendous potential passion offers them. As *FedEx* employees will attest, work becomes fun and rewarding when it draws on individual passions."
~Frederick W. Smith, founder of *Federal Express*

"The biggest mistake people make in life is not trying to make a living at doing what they most enjoy. Success follows doing what you want to do. There is no other way to be successful."
~Malcolm S. Forbes, CEO of *Forbes Magazine*

"I got C's all through high school and I was a very lazy student. It wasn't until I got out of college that I applied myself and became very successful, because I found my passion. When you have a passion it makes a big difference."
~Linda Keeler, General Manager of *Sony Pictures*

"All we know for sure is there's a connection between enthusiasm and motivation that allows you to get energized from an activity that would otherwise take energy from somebody else. This, my friends, is what I refer to as a passion -- something that gives you more energy than it takes and is uniquely fascinating to you. Anyone who sets out to build something great around a passion will need a massive amount of energy to continue developing the skills to make it happen. That's why most people fail. It's not because they don't have the raw ability, it's because they are simply doing things that don't give them energy. And without that energy, you can't build the necessary skill set fast enough to accomplish what you want to." ~Tom Bilyeu, founder of *Quest Bar and Impact Theory*

"If you don't love what you do, then you shouldn't do it... If you don't have emotion and you don't have passion, then you shouldn't be in business, because money is the byproduct and not the purpose. When selecting businesses, I first have to be enticed by the product or the industry they are in. Then I look for passion. If a company has these two qualifiers, I go for it."
~Marcus Lemonis

"If you're not following your passion you'll always be looking for an exit."
~T. Harv Eker

"Too many companies believe people are interchangeable. Truly gifted people never are. They have unique talents. Such people cannot be forced into roles they are not suited for, nor should they be. Effective leaders allow great people to do the work they were born to do."

~Warren Bennis from *Organizing Genius*

Chapter Three
Staffing for Talent

The second critical element of a *Strengths Oriented Staffing* strategy is **TALENT**. Similar concepts are aptitude, inborn ability, potential, gifting, knack, flair, bent, instinct, genius, inclination, brilliance and forte. Talent is what applicants are naturally good at. And to paraphrase Lady Gaga, "*Baby They Were Born This Way*". Talents are innate and enduring.

The late *Gallup* leader Don O. Clifton writes, "Talents naturally occur within you and cannot be acquired. They are inborn predispositions. They are things that you do instinctively." And Marcus Buckingham adds, "Talent is a naturally recurring pattern of thought, feeling, or behavior that can be productively applied."

In her book *Multipliers,* Liz Wiseman explains, "A native genius is something that people do, not only exceptionally well, but absolutely naturally. They do it easily (without extra effort) and freely (without condition). What people do easily, they do without conscious effort. They do it better than anything else they do, but they don't need to apply extraordinary effort to the task. It is effortless, and they stand ready and willing to contribute, whether it is a formal job requirement or not. Finding someone's native genius is the key that unlocks discretionary effort. It propels people to go beyond what is required and offer their full intelligence. Finding people's genius begins by carefully observing them in action, looking for spikes of authentic enthusiasm and a natural flow of energy."

These talents give each person a special ability to do certain kinds of tasks easily and happily, yet also make other tasks seem like pure torture. Can you imagine comedian Robin Williams trying to work as an accountant?"

Talents are inborn or innate. Talents are instinctual. Talents are natural. When an employee uses a talent, they might experience what I call a **"made for this moment"**. They might get a sense that they were made or born to do that activity.

Using talents, like breathing, may seem almost effortless. At least it feels easy. That doesn't mean a worker doesn't need to work hard at building on their talent, but it might feel like they're not working as hard.

Talents often show up early in life although there is frequently not an adult around who is paying attention.

Rapid learning is a strong sign of talent. Results or success are a sign of talent. By learning how to hire for talent, instead of just skills, your training costs will drop and your employee will succeed bigger and faster. As *Container Store* founder Kip Tindell says, "One Great Employee = Three Good Employees." Discovering talent will help you hire that "One Great Employee".

Dilbert is a very successful comic strip written by Scott Adams. He regularly lampoons what's ridiculous about corporate America. A few years back, a TV cartoon series was developed based on the Dilbert character.

There is a great clip from one of the episodes circulating on *YouTube* that perfectly gives an example of what I'm talking about when I use the term "talent path". In the clip, Dilbert's mom takes him to the doctor with a concern about his habit of tearing mechanical devices apart around the house. He had just disassembled the television, a clock and a stereo and then used the components to build a ham radio set. (I hear stories like this all the time in my classes.)

The doctor shares with Dilbert's mom that he has a rare condition called *"The Knack"*. "The Knack," continues the doctor, "is a rare condition characterized by all things mechanical and electrical... and utter social ineptitude. He won't be able to lead a normal life... in fact he will be forced to become an engineer."

I'm convinced that every applicant that comes into your system has "The Knack" although it may have absolutely nothing to do with mechanical aptitudes. Their "Knack" may be with music, marketing, ministry or any one of 10,000 other things.

Generically their knack will include *Aptitude* Talents, *Activity* Talents and *Approach* Talents forming what I call the Talent Triangle. Again, whether you are reading this book to help select candidates for a job, shape an existing job or maximize their success in a current job, think about ways to help them combine their talents and mix them with their passion.

Candidate Aptitude Talents

Aptitudes are underlying drivers of unique ability. I believe they are connected with individualized areas of intelligence. *Harvard* professor, Howard Gardner has done extensive research with Savants, those with brain injuries and people who have succeeded wildly, but often in very narrow niches. He concludes that there are ability specific regions of the brain, and therefore multiple intelligences or aptitudes in up to nine areas. He suggests that most people have not one intelligence or set of aptitudes but a unique blend or hierarchy of several including:

Word Aptitudes
Number/Logic Aptitudes
Picture Aptitudes
Music Aptitudes
Body Aptitudes
People Aptitudes
Self Awareness Aptitudes

Gardner says we should <u>not be asking</u>, "How smart is this individual?" Rather we <u>should be asking</u>, "How is this individual smart?"

The *Johnson O'Connor Foundation* grew out of aptitude and job fit research at *General Electric*. For career selection assessments, it may be one of the most helpful. They use work sample tests, which tend to be the most accurate. However, they no longer conduct pre-employment assessments.

Johnson O'Connor accesses for 19 or 20 aptitudes including:

Personality – Preference for working in groups or alone
Graphoria – Clerical ability with figures and symbols
Ideaphoria – Fluency of ideas
Structural Visualization – Ability to think in 3 dimensions
Abstract Visualization – Ability to work with ideas
Inductive Reasoning – See connections in scattered facts
Analytical Reasoning – Separating into component parts
Finger Dexterity – Manipulating fingers skillfully
Tweezer Dexterity - Handling small tools easily
Observation – Taking careful notice
Design Memory – Memorizing designs rapidly
Tonal Memory – Remembering sounds and music notes
Pitch Discrimination – Differentiate musical tones
Rhythmic Ability – Ability to keep time
Timbre Discrimination – Detect sounds of same pitch & volume
Number Memory – Remembering numbers of all kinds
Proportional Appraisal – Discerning harmonious designs
Silograms – Ability to learn languages and technical jargon
Foresight – Look into the future with wisdom
Color Perception – Distinguish colors

The *Johnson O'Connor Laboratory* has also measured eye dominance, physical energy, taste for sour and vocabulary.

O*NET – Abilities

Abilities - Enduring attributes of the individual that influence performance.

O*NET is a website run by the *Department of Labor* and it has a lot of good information that can help both candidates and companies better understand aptitudes, activities and how they connect with different work roles. *The Handbook of Human Abilities – Definitions, Measurements and Job Task Requirements*, written by Edwin A. Fleishman and Maureen E. Reilly appears to be the source document for much of the information. The website has short definitions of each ability listed below. To see these along with definitions of each go to the *O*NET* website:
https://www.onetonline.org/find/descriptor/browse/Abilities/

Cognitive	Physical	Psychomotor	Sensory
Category Flexibility	Dynamic Flexibility	Arm-Hand Steadiness	Auditory Attention
Deductive Reasoning	Dynamic Strength	Control Precision	Depth Perception
Flexibility of Closure	Explosive Strength	Finger Dexterity	Far Vision
Fluency of Ideas	Extent Flexibility	Manual Dexterity	Glare Sensitivity
Inductive Reasoning	Gross Body Coord.	Multi-Limb Coordination	Hearing Sensitivity
Information Ordering	Gross Body Equilib.	Rate Control	Near Vision
Mathematical Reasoning	Stamina	Reaction Time	Night Vision
Memorization	Static Strength	Response Orientation	Peripheral Vision
Number Facility	Trunk Strength	Speed of Limb Movement	Sound Location
Oral Comprehension		Wrist-Finder Speed	Speech Clarity
Originality			Speech Recognition
Perceptual Speed			Color Discrimination
Problem Sensitivity			
Selective Attention			
Spatial Orientation			
Speed of Closure			
Time Sharing			
Visualization			
Written Comprehension			
Written Expression			

Candidate Activity Talents

The candidate's **Activity Talents** will often fall into **Four Types** or often a combination of type preferences.

The four include:

Working with People

Advise, Analyze, Build, Coach, Coordinate, Develop, Direct, Evaluate, Help, Inform, Inspire, Interview, Lead, Manage, Motivate, Observe, Organize, Persuade, Recruit, Rehabilitate, Research, Select, Serve, Sketch, Supervise, Teach, Test, Train, Unite

Working with Things

Adapt, Analyze, Arrange, Assemble, Balance, Budget, Build, Classify, Clean, Collect, Cook, Create, Deliver, Design, Diagnose, Display, Distribute, Drive, Estimate, Examine, Fix, Grow, Imagine, Improve, Inspect, Install, Invent, Inventory, Maintain, Operate, Paint, Photograph, Promote, Restore, Select, Sell, Sew, Set Up, Show, Sketch, Test, Weigh

Working with Ideas

Analyze, Arrange, Assemble, Brainstorm, Classify, Collect, Communicate, Connect, Create, Describe, Design, Develop, Discover, Display, Dramatize, Edit, Expand, Experiment, Express, File, Fix, Illustrate, Imagine, Implement, Improve, Improvise, Manage, Promote, Question, Recommend, Research, Sell, Shape, Share, Study, Summarize, Synergize, Systemize, Teach, Test

Working with Data or Information

Analyze, Arrange, Classify, Check, Collect, Communicate, Consolidate, Discover, Dissect, Edit, Explain, File, Illustrate, Interpret, Investigate, Log, Manage, Memorize, Organize, Protect, Question, Read, Research, Restore, Retrieve, Sell, Sort, Study, Summarize, Synthesize, Systemize, Test, Transcribe, Understand

That's a start, but you'll want to get even more granular in your staff-awareness and which activities the candidates are attracted to.

Candidate Approach Talents

To explain the difference between Approach Talents and Activities or Aptitudes, let's consider comedians and crime fighters. First let's imagine you're hiring a comedian.

The job of a comedian or comic is to make people laugh. That is a talent or aptitude. But there are many approaches to that talent. Some of the approaches are related to a particular medium, but even within a single medium, there are many approaches.

You may make people laugh as a comedic actor, a comedy writer, a comic strip creator or a stand-up comedian. As a comic strip creator, you may have the gift for a single panel or multi-panel strip. You might have the ability to do both, but it's likely you'll be better at one or the other. And then consider the content and style of the strip. Could *Peanuts* creator Charles Schultz produce in the style of *Far Side* creator Gary Larson? I doubt it. Even within a single medium, their "Approaches" to comic strip humor are vastly different.

Consider "Approaches" to stand-up comedy. My favorite comedians include the quiet, slow talking Steven Wright and the zany maniacal Robin Williams. They both make me laugh. But their approaches to stand-up comedy are worlds apart. Make a list of 10 people that make you laugh. It's the same result, but not one of them will do it exactly the same way. Some are extremely gifted with physical comedy. That is, they use their body. With others, like Jim Carrey, it's facial expressions. Some tell a long story with a device called the "running gag". The late Johnny Carson had a way of getting laughs from his response to his jokes that didn't get laughs. When his topical humor sagged, he got funnier. Jerry Seinfeld's observational humor digs deeply into the minutia of everyday life.

Now imagine you're hiring a crime fighter or super hero? What makes them interesting isn't their crime fighting. What makes them interesting is how they do it. They all fight crime. Essentially they get the same results. The bad guys lose. But they all use a completely unique set of talents or powers. Superman, Batman, Green Hornet, Hulk, Spiderman, Wonder Woman and Thor are all very different in their approach. But each one has discovered, developed and delivers a set of strengths that are unique to them. And so should you. What's your super power?

If you would like a terrific assessment to help you identify your "Approach Talents", I recommend *Gallup's Strengthsfinder 2.0* which helps you identify a unique hierarchy of 34 Approaches to any activity. Each of the 34 Approaches is classified under four Types including: **Executing, Influencing, Relationship Building and Strategic Thinking.** *Strengthsfinder 2.0* then gets more detailed or more granular. Each theme has underlying threads that explains the domain.

Executing Type	Influencing Type	Relating Type	Strategic Thinking Type
Achiever	Activator	Adaptability	Analytical
Arranger	Command	Developer	Context
Belief	Communication	Connectedness	Futuristic
Consistency	Competition	Empathy	Ideation
Deliberate	Maximizer	Harmony	Input
Discipline	Self-Assurance	Includer	Intellection
Focus	Significance	Individualization	Learner
Responsibility	Woo	Positivity	Strategic
Restorative		Relator	

Note: Each of the 34 Strengthsfinder Themes are registered trademarks of *The Gallup Organization*. It should be noted that they have developed their own definitions and language of strengths that may vary slightly from dictionary definitions.

*O*NET* refers to a similar list of Approach Talents as Work Styles. To see that list go to: https://www.onetonline.org/find/descriptor/browse/Work_Styles/

Hiring For Talent at *Facebook*

When *Facebook's* VP of People, Lori Goler was beginning as a manager for a startup in 1999, she picked up a copy of the newly released guide to management, *First, Break All the Rules*. The book, authored by *Gallup* analysts Marcus Buckingham and Curt Coffman become a fast bestseller. In an interview with *Business Insider*, Goler said, "It really struck a chord with me."

When joining *Facebook* as its head of Human Resources in 2008, she immediately adapted Buckingham and Coffman's teachings to the company, turning it into a "strengths-based" organization.

Since then, Buckingham has consulted extensively with *Facebook*. And when an employee becomes a manager at *Facebook*, "First, Break All the Rules" comes as highly recommended reading.

Buckingham and Coffman based their book on 25 years of *Gallup* studying 80,000 managers across 400 companies. They found that the best performing companies had managers who "broke all the rules" by flouting conventional wisdom in four key ways:

• Great managers **select for talent** . . . not simply experience, intelligence, or determination.
• Great managers **define the right outcomes** . . . not the right steps.
• Great managers **focus on strengths** . . . not weaknesses.
• Great managers help associates **find the right fit** . . . not simply the next rung on the ladder.

In summary, the best managers don't hire and promote with the intention of shaping employees. Instead, they give them more opportunities to develop what they've proven they're already good at.

Buckingham and Coffman argue, "Organizations that aren't strength-based promote employees to their level of incompetence, making them unhappy and less effective in the process." This explains why at *Facebook*, the job of manager isn't viewed as a promotion but as an alternate career path. Goler says, "The company selects managers who actually *want* to be managers… It sounds basic, but it's harder than it sounds in an organization that's scaling quickly."

Goler concludes, "People want to have an impact; they want to know that what they're working on matters. And they're going to stay at a place where they feel like they have an impact, [where] they're learning and growing and doing work they love."

More Thoughts on Talent

"I worked out what I was good at and what I was bad at. It became pretty clear what I wanted to do. I was really only interested in design. I was neither interested, or good at building a business."
~Jonathan Ive, *Apple* Design Team Leader

"No two persons are born exactly alike; but each differs from the other in natural endowments, one being suited for one occupation and the other for another."
~Plato (427-347 BC) Classical Greek Philosopher and Mathematician

"Personality style is the way a person acts when he or she is able to do things his or her own way. Most people are consistent enough in their behavior to allow you to predict their behavior."

~Kate Ward, Author, *Personality Style at Work*

Chapter Four
Staffing for Personality

The third element of selecting great people is **PERSONALITY** or temperament. You might think of a candidate's personality style as a kind of map that suggests both the inner geography and the outward direction of their life. Whether they know it or not, to some extent, they follow its path every single day of their life.

We all spend a great deal of time assessing the personalities and temperaments of others. In a basic sense, it is simply getting to know, understand and then describe someone. As soon as we begin to describe a person, we generally use trait, temperament and personality language to do it.

People generally behave in patterned, organized and recognizable ways. If we say that someone is outgoing, we usually mean that they are outgoing with some degree of regularity. A pattern is implied. With some consistency, we can also say that some traits often come packaged together in a somewhat unique, yet similar and discernible grouping that we might call a personality type.

The evidence is strong that our personality comes from at least three places:

Nature – A candidate's temperament is innate and natural from birth. These traits often show up as early as infancy and nearly always as toddlers.

Nurture - It is also influenced or shaped by environment, family, culture and friends.

Choice - Personality is a combined set of behaviors that to some extent can be expressed at will. For example, I am naturally reserved, but I can choose to be gregarious and outgoing when the occasion calls for it. But it doesn't come naturally and I expend a tremendous amount of energy to do it.

Everyone seems to have patterns and natural preferences that can be observed.

Personalities can be described in terms of individual traits. Some personality psychologists explain them as a position on an axis or line between opposites. Examples are:

- Intense or Relaxed?
- Shy or Outgoing?
- Fast or Slow?
- Options-open or Decisive?
- Analytical or Active?
- Independent or Dependent?
- Extroverted or Introverted?
- Leader or Follower?
- Flexible or Structured?

Some of the above traits are inextricably attached to the level of success your applicants will achieve in a given role! Some roles may optimize if a candidate has paradoxical or complimentary traits. It's worth your time to figure out the connections.

Often personality traits show up in groups. Those natural groupings have led to numerous sorting systems.

There are three different personality sorting systems that I have studied and use with clients and all three have applications to hiring. The three systems include:

- *D.I.S.C.*
- *Myers-Briggs*

• *Meta-Programs* from *Neuro-Linguistic Programming*

Never allow any assessment to define a candidate with a declarative statement. But personality assessments can give you "hints" or "clues" that offer self-discovery insight. To maximize assessment results, make sure you ask the candidate to customize the report. Have them highlight the descriptions that describe them best. In some cases you may ask that they have a partner or close friend read over the report and offer feedback. Ask them to re-write any inaccurate description so that it precisely portrays their personality. Realize that everyone can learn to "**play in all the rooms**". Some rooms will just be more comfortable.

The *D.I.S.C.* Profile

In this book, I only cover *DISC*. The *DISC* Profile is the most popular assessment used by organizations worldwide. Over 50 million people have used the instrument to communicate better and understand their talents and non-talents. *DISC* first came to prominence in the military - it was widely used as part of the *US Army's* recruitment process during the years leading to the *Second World War*. Having proved its value, it gradually came to be used in a business recruitment setting. Although the history goes all the way back to Hippocrates, around 500 B.C., the modern assessment was first developed by psychologist William Marston who was a very interesting man. He was also the inventor of the lie-detector test and the superhero *Wonder Woman*. Marston never attempted to copyright the assessment, so today, slightly different versions are produced by different vendors.

DISC starts with only four basic behavior types, naturally grouping several dozen traits that commonly show up together.

Each letter in *DISC* represents a different trait grouping. The four types combine into thousands of possible patterns reflecting the complexity of human strengths. Sophisticated reports show up to 28 personality blends.

How I Use *D.I.S.C.*

- Suggest Potential Job Matches
- Identify Job Search Challenges
- Use In Building Interview Strategies
- Training Leaders and Managers

D.I.S.C Style Overview

Direct	**Interactive**
Direct	Interacting
Directive	Influencing
Doer	Inducing
Determined	Inspiring
Decisive	Initiating
Destination	Inclusive
Daring	Instigating
Dominant	Immediate
Driving	Inviting
Problem Area-Demanding	Problem Area-Impulsive
Conceptual	**Stabilizing**
Conceptual	Stabilizing
Conscientious	Steadying
Cautious	Sincere
Calculating	Supporting
Consistent	Standardizing
Classifying	Sympathetic
Compliant	Social Sameness
Contemplating	Sacrificial
Controlled	Serving
Problem Area-Critical	Problem Area-Slow

It's not a perfect tool. **Everyone has a little of each style**. To get a quick sense of your own special blend, read each of the descriptors in the four categories and assign a number 1-10 (10 meaning it very much describes you) for how much the word describes you.

Dan Harrison offers an assessment that looks at over 170 traits and attempts to measure the paradoxical ones mentioned earlier. So if you are looking for a candidate that is both bold and sensitive, a very rare grouping in my experience, that might be a good option for you.

In an interview with *LinkedIn*, *Virgin* founder Richard Branson says he focuses on personality as a key factor. Branson shares, "The first thing to look for when searching for a great employee is somebody with a personality that fits with your company culture. Most skills can be learned, but it is difficult to train people on their personality. If you can find people who are fun, friendly, caring and love helping others, you are on to a winner. Personality is the key. It is not something that always comes out in an interview – people can be shy. But you have to trust your judgment. If you are interviewing a slightly introverted person with a great personality, use your experience to pull it out of them. It is easier with an extrovert, but be wary of people becoming overexcited in the pressure of interviews."

More Thoughts on Personality

"When I commanded the 2nd Brigade of the 101st Airborne Division, I had several gifted commanders with radically different personalities. I could tell one to go take a hill, and it was done. I could tell another to go take a hill and he immediately asked questions: 'When? How? What other support can you give me? Do I have priority on resources? Then what do I do?' Both commanders would take the hill and accomplish the mission. Who was the better commander? The can-do commander was exciting and admirable, but he sometimes charged off without asking basic questions. He could get in trouble quickly. He did not always capture all my guidance and the larger picture of the battlefield. The other commander could annoy me with his pestering questions, but he often came up with a more skillful plan and more careful execution. My job was to get the best out of both and complement their strengths and shortcomings."
~Colin Powell, U.S. Secretary of State

"My biggest mistake is probably weighing too much on someone's talent and not someone's personality."
~Elon Musk, founder of *Tesla*

"Your personality is your preferred way of engaging with your world around you. Your personality is who you are on auto-pilot. Your personality is your natural state. Your personality is your spontaneous behaviors."
~Reggie McNeal, Author, *Get A Life*

"Make sure your values and the values of the organization are compatible."

~Peter F. Drucker

Chapter Five
Staffing for Values

"Make sure your values and the values of the organization are compatible."
~Peter F. Drucker

A candidate's **VALUES** include their ideals, what's important to them, what they care about, what drives them and what motivates them. If they value a method, a person or object, that means they appreciate and respect them. **Values, when they are aligned, form a group's culture**. The candidate's personal DNA should match the organizational DNA with regard to values.

If a candidate has a rule, a standard or an ideal, behind it you will find a value. When they use the word "should" there is almost always a value behind it. Families have values. Churches have values. Community service groups have values. Corporations have values. Countries and even regions of the country have values. All individuals have values.

In America, our founding fathers held a clear set of values that shaped what we were to become. Some of those values included freedom, equality under the law, justice, choice, opportunity, representation, presumption of innocence, right to trial before a jury of peers, individuality, the pursuit of happiness. They were spelled out in documents like the *Declaration of Independence, The Constitution* and *The Bill of Rights*.

All companies have values with regard to things like product quality, speed, beauty, service, customer experience and price point. And in reality they have these values in a sequence, hierarchy or order. No company values these ideals equally.

In general, a candidate's values are a type of strength that will align with the organization and team they are working with. Value conflicts create a culture where employees aren't working together.

In the book *ROADMAP*, Nathan Gebhard, Brian MacAllister and Mike Marriner talk about the difference between "Truths" and "Subjective Truths".

"Truths"	"Subjective Truths"
Without water we die	I want to make a lot of money
Camels have three eyelids	I work best when I'm my own boss
Karaoke = "empty orchestra" in Japanese	I hate big cities

Values are subjective truths. They include our unique needs for achievement, independence, recognition, relationships, support or special working conditions. Values often are tied to the rewards people seek. Some people value money, others want intellectual challenges, and still others desire prestige or a comfortable lifestyle. People with the similar talents and passion may pursue very different careers based on their values.

Values came on the scene as a topic of serious study in 1914. German philosopher and psychologist Eduard Spranger published *Types of Men: the Psychology and Ethics of Personality*. Spranger described his research and observations concluding that six core values were found present in every person. He believed those values were what created drive and motivation.

An American Psychologist named Gordon Allport picked up on Spranger's work beginning in the 1950's. Allport believed that a person's personality type was connected to their values. I tend to agree with Allport on this and I would add that individual talent and passion is connected as well. For that reason, I believe that values have some biological or innate basis. In my thinking, values are less dynamic and not quite as influenced by environment or nurture as many would speculate.

In general, a candidate's values are a type of strength that should align with the organization they are applying into. If you place a high value on customer experience and service but you work for an organization that doesn't, you won't be happy at work. The possible exception is if you are brought into an organization specifically to orchestrate a change in values. This is quite different than talent and personality strengths where a wide variety might be desirable. But with values, the organization is usually better off if everyone is on the same page (or a page nearby).

There are literally hundreds of potential values I could list. But I'm going to introduce this in a simple useable format.

Here is a list of values I often use as a starting point in my strengths clarification work.

I developed the acronym **M.Y. B.I.G. D.R.I.V.E.R.S.** as a memory aid:

Mastery - Growth, Development, Progress, Maturity
Yield - Money, Economic, Reward, Return, Compensation

Beauty – Aesthetics, Form, Artistic Expression
Influence – Authority, Control, Power
Giving – Service, Altruism, Helping

Discovery – Theory, Knowledge, Understanding, Truth
Regulatory – Structure, Order, Routine, Sameness
Individualistic - Independent, Uniqueness, Autonomy
Variety – Change, Newness, Innovation, Creativity
Excellence – Quality, Craftsmanship, Superiority
Relationships – Co-Workers, Collaboration, Teamwork
Safety – Security, Protection, Guarantees

Have a candidate ponder these 12 value themes and threads. Ask them to put them in order according to their own hierarchy. Ask them to resist ordering them based on how they think they *should* be ordered. Then try to do the same with the company.

Many top companies are focusing much more heavily on hiring people with matching values. This is smart from a hiring perspective. It's really difficult and time consuming to change a person's values. And the same is true for you. Your chances of shifting a company's value set or culture will probably be an exercise in futility, a complete waste of time. Trust me on this. I've tried.

Some of these values may be important to a candidate in one place or context but not in another. For example, beauty may be very important to them at home but only moderately important at work. So when you're trying to clarify a candidate's values, it's important that you think about a single context. A value may be universal but it also may be very specific to a particular environment.

Also, any list of values or values assessment report may make a candidate think of an important value that is not on the list. If that's the case, explore it. They may also think of a word that means the same as those listed, but for some reason a different word has more power for them. Have them use their own words but also help them understand the unique language of the organization.

More Thoughts on Values

"All decision-making is a values clarifying exercise."
~Tony Robbins, Author and Speaker

"It's very important for people to know themselves and understand what their value system is, because if you don't know what your value system is, then you don't know what risks are worth taking and which ones are worth avoiding."
~Ben Carson, Surgeon

"A leader will find it difficult to articulate a coherent vision unless it expresses his core values, his basic identity... one must first embark on the formidable journey of self-discovery in order to create a vision with authentic soul."
~Mihaly Csikszentmihalyi, Psychologist, Author of *Flow*

"The founders of great, enduring organizations like *Hewlett-Packard, 3M*, and *Johnson & Johnson* often did not have a vision statement when they started out. They usually began with a set of strong personal core values and a relentless drive for progress and had—most important—a remarkable ability to translate these into concrete mechanisms…**You cannot 'set' organizational values, you can only discover them. Nor can you 'install' new core values into people. Core values are not something people 'buy in' to. People must be predisposed to holding them.** Executives often ask me, 'How do we get people to share our core values?' You don't. Instead, the task is to *find* people who are already predisposed to sharing your core values. You must attract and then retain these people and let those who aren't predisposed to sharing your core values go elsewhere."
~Jim Collins, Business Consultant, Author of *Good to Great*

"You have to decide what your priorities truly are – what it is that is truly important to you. What does success look like to you? What do you really stand for and where do you spend your time, energy and money? For example, among the things I value most in my life are my personal relationship with Jesus Christ; providing for, protecting and nurturing my family; my health; and being a responsible contributing member of society."
~Dr. Phil McGraw, Psychologist and TV Personality

"Those people who develop the ability to continuously acquire new and better forms of knowledge that they can apply to their work and to their lives will be the movers and shakers in our society for the indefinite future."

~Brian Tracy, Author and Speaker

Chapter Six
Staffing for Knowledge

The next step on your Staff Path is **KNOWLEDGE**. It often builds synergy with skill as it works on top of the talent/passion foundation. Where skill is about mastering methods, steps and sequences; knowledge is about terminology, principles, policies, rules, information, concepts, theories and facts. In a strengths context, knowledge can be described as an organized body of information, often of a factual nature and sometimes of a procedural nature. It would be information that would make performing a certain type of work possible.

As an example of pure knowledge, I keep three resources in my library. One is a construction dictionary. It has 648 pages of construction oriented terminology. It doesn't show me how to build a thing. That would move into skills, a separate but related skill dimension. It would help me communicate with tradesmen more accurately.

The second is a copy of the *Uniform Building Code*. This is a set of building rules and regulations designed to keep us all safe in the event of an earthquake or other catastrophe. Again, this resource is very knowledge oriented and doesn't move into building skills.

I also own a pocket dictionary of art terms. It doesn't help me paint or draw or sculpt. It would help me communicate with artists.

In his terrific book, *Now, Discover Your Strengths*, Marcus Buckingham explains, "You need factual knowledge, which is content. For example, when you start to learn a language, factual knowledge is the vocabulary. In the same vein, salespeople must spend time learning their product features. Pilots must learn call signal protocols. Nurses must know exactly how much *Novocain* is appropriate for each procedure. No matter what your skills or talents you won't excel at painting if you don't know that red and green paint, when combined, create the color brown. Factual knowledge such as this gets you in the game. The second kind of knowledge is experiential, which isn't taught in classrooms or found in manuals. Rather it is something you must discipline yourself to pick up along the way and retain."

Knowledge can also be divided up into basic knowledge, working knowledge and detailed knowledge. Hire people who have knowledge, but more importantly, hire people who have a strong thirst for knowledge in the area they are being hired!

Basic Knowledge

Basic knowledge includes the types of information found in a source document, or knowledge of the general types of information covered in a specific subject field. Basic knowledge will allow you to use a source to find specific information when it is needed. For example, a general knowledge of *STRENGTHSPATH* strengths would help you know where to look for more knowledge of a certain type. A basic knowledge of baseball might refer to a general understanding of the rules, their purposes, the general subjects the rules cover and where to reference the rules.

Working Knowledge

Working knowledge includes general knowledge plus knowledge of, and ability to recall important and commonly used information from the source. For example, a general working of strengths would include the general knowledge mentioned above, and also the ability to recall major commonly held ideas from the strengths movement and specific strengths practitioners. A working knowledge of baseball might include the tendencies of a particular player, team or manager and their strategy in a particular situation.

Detailed Knowledge

Detailed knowledge is thorough knowledge of all information contained in a source or set of sources. Using the strengths example again, a strengths coach or strengths practitioner would be expected to have detailed knowledge of a variety of strategies and methods to help a client, student or group discover, develop, describe and deliver their strengths in the workplace without having to look them up. This would include strategies and methods that are not frequently used. A detailed knowledge of baseball would allow you to manage, coach or otherwise oversee practices and games.

Some things you can learn from a textbook, a class, an online program, a parent or a friend. You can acquire knowledge through study and reflection. Some types of knowledge require experience. There are some things you just can't get out of a book. There are some things you can learn but you really can't be taught. Most of our education system is designed to impart knowledge, often in the form of rote memorization with very little explanation of how it relates to real life.

To excel or become world class in any given field, you will need to develop expertise. In other words you will need to become extremely knowledgeable in the area you want to work.

Terminology (Descriptions)

Every profession has a unique language that includes vocabulary, terminology, names for parts and pieces, as well as names for equipment and tools. Medical workers have to learn medical terminology. Construction workers have to learn construction terminology.

Location

If you are a doctor, you will need to learn where each body part is located. If you are a lawyer, you may need to learn how the law library is organized and where to look for case decisions and legal precedents. If you are an information technology specialist, you need to learn where the computer components are located and how they fit together.

*O*NET* Knowledge List

Knowledge - Organized sets of principles and facts applying in general domains:

Business & Management	Manufacturing & Production	Engineering and Technology
Administration Management Clerical Economics Accounting Sales Marketing Customer Service Personal Service Personnel and Human Resources	Production Processing Food Production Agriculture **Education & Training** Education Training Coaching	Computers Electronics Engineering Technology Design Building and Construction Mechanical
Health Services Medicine Dentistry Therapy Counseling	**Arts and Humanities** English Language Foreign Language Fine Arts Theater History Archeology Philosophy Theology	**Math and Science** Mathematics Physics Chemistry Biology Psychology Sociology Anthropology Geography
Law and Public Safety Public Safety and Security Law and Government Civil Law Criminal Law		**Communications** Telecommunications Communications Media Social Media Film Television
Transportation Air Transportation Road Transportation Air Transportation		

Understanding

Every profession involves pattern recognition, rules, principles, symptoms, and meaning along with cause and effect relationships. Knowledge allows you to create "distinctions". When I look inside a computer I say, "Yep, it's a computer." Hopefully, when my repairperson at the *Genius Bar* looks, he or she knows with great precision exactly what each piece is and what it does. Distinction leads to accurate diagnostics. These aren't developable skills so much as they are about building an essential knowledge base.

Professional football players spend an incredible amount of time watching game film. This is not to build their skill. They are expanding their knowledge. When they watch film of themselves they are expanding self-awareness. They also watch film of the teams they will be playing to learn patterns and tendencies.

Whatever work you choose, you will need to develop an awareness and a level of understanding of systems, procedures, equipment, theories, rules, laws, codes, precedents and more.

The Knowledge To Get More Knowledge

In a world of accelerated knowledge and rapid change, life-long learning becomes a high priority. Learning how to learn is paramount!

Knowledge and Truth

Many, including some in the scientific field confuse knowledge and truth. The truth never really changes. 2 + 2 = 4. It will always equal 4. That is truth. Knowledge advances, expands and even changes. Prior to this writing, 2 elements have been added to the Periodic Table. I grew up with the knowledge that Pluto is one of 9 planets in our solar system. Scientists are now suggesting otherwise. Pluto has been demoted to "Dwarf Planet" status. But not so fast. The controversy continues.

General Knowledge

Thomas Edison famously used a general knowledge questionnaire when hiring applicants. I've studied Edison's rational and I'm not sure I fully understand or agree with its use for hiring across all positions. It could be useful for hiring for positions where the candidate would be more valuable if they needed to communicate with a wide variety of people. Edison's questionnaire was 146 questions long. Here are the first 10 questions:

1. What countries bound France?

2. What city and country produce the finest china?

3. Where is the River Volga?

4. What is the finest cotton grown?

5. What country consumed the most tea before the war?

6. What city in the United States leads in making laundry machines?

7. What city is the fur centre of the United States?

8. What country is the greatest textile producer?

9. Is Australia greater than Greenland in area?

10. Where is Copenhagen?

To view the whole questionnaire with answers try this link:
http://www.openculture.com/2015/03/thomas-edisons-146-question-knowledge-test-for-prospective-employees.html

More Thoughts on Knowledge

"A fork in the road for most careers is what we choose to do when we confront a vocabulary (from finance, technology, psychology, literature...) that we don't understand. We can either demand that people dumb down their discourse (and fall behind) or we can learn the words. It's hard to be a doctor or an engineer or key grip if you don't know what the words mean, because learning the words is the same thing as learning the concepts."
~Seth Godin, Author and Marketing Expert

"Research is creating new knowledge."
~Neil Armstrong, Astronaut

"Knowledge has to be improved, challenged, and increased constantly, or it vanishes...Today knowledge has power. It controls access to opportunity and advancement."
~Peter Drucker, Management Consultant

"Those people who develop the ability to continuously acquire new and better forms of knowledge that they can apply to their work and to their lives will be the movers and shakers in our society for the indefinite future."
~Brian Tracy, Author and Speaker

"To acquire knowledge, one must study; but to acquire wisdom, one must observe."
~Marilyn vos Savant, World's Highest I.Q.

"There is no substitute for accurate knowledge. Know yourself, know your business, know your men."
~Lee Iacocca, former *Chrysler* C.E.O.

"Experts have their knowledge in order. When your knowledge is not in order, the more confused you become by definition."
~Nido Qubein, Author and Speaker

"Everyone has a chance to learn, improve, and build up their skills."

~Tom Peters, Excellence in Business Consultant

Chapter Seven
Staffing for Skills

Most companies hire for **SKILLS**, often exclusively. Many companies now refer to them as competencies and the whole hiring and selection process is geared toward understanding this aspect of a candidate's strengths. It's not that skills aren't important, they are. Skill discovery is geared toward uncovering the questions, "Can this person do the job?" and sometimes, "How well can this person do the job?" The problem is that a singular focus on this category overlooks more fundamental questions, "Does this person want to do the job?" – "Will this person look forward to doing the job?" – "Will this person fully engage with the job?" – or… "Will this person just be clocking hours, waiting for the weekend?"

While the first four strength dimensions tend to have a natural, innate or genetic basis, the skills are primarily developed. This dimension of a candidate's *STRENGTHSPATH* are their developed abilities, mastery, proficiencies, competencies, know-how and how-to, including methods, steps, order, sequences, strategies, tactics and proficiencies with tools and technologies. Skills are abilities developed through deliberate systematic effort, intentional practice and often supported by role models, mentoring, training and coaching. **Skills are what you add to talents in order to transform them into deliverable strengths**.

While talents are innate and enduring, skills are developed over time. In his book, *What's Your Genius?*, Jay Niblick talks about what he calls

"The Simple Mistake". Jay describes a major problem in our culture when he writes, "The vast majority of people assume there is no real difference between talents and skills. They fail to appreciate just how fixed the neural networks that control these talents really are."

Corporate selection expert Jim Barrett frames this discussion by talking about the difference between aptitude and ability. Barrett writes, "Aptitude should not be confused with abilities. Present skills and capabilities are not aptitudes. Aptitudes are about potential, which is not necessarily realized at the present time."

Jim and Jay are correct. Innate, inborn, natural talent is the underlying foundation of successful performance. But they are different from skills, which must be developed or learned. That doesn't mean skills aren't important. They are a critical component of your strength mosaic. I don't know about you, but I don't want a "naturally talented" doctor who hasn't gone to medical school or had lengthy internship, ad-libbing through my abdomen.

Hire for skills, but more importantly, hire for skills that are well-supported by underlying natural talents!

One reason for the confusion between talent and skill is they often are used interchangeably. We can say that someone is a skilled musician and we can also say that same person is a talented musician. But they really refer to two very different pieces to the puzzle. Again, talent you are born with and skills are something you develop and add to the talent in order to turn it into a strength.

Another reason for the confusion is that there are those in our culture who still believe natural talent doesn't exist. There are those who believe that with enough practice and hard work, anyone can do anything. But the science and the evidence just will not support that.

Math requires some knowledge. But much of mathematics is a skill. Basic arithmetic skills are adding, subtracting, multiplying and dividing. Computing ratios, rates and percentages is basically skill oriented, although it does require some knowledge. The practical application of fractions, percentages, ratios and proportions, logarithms, slide rule, practical algebra, geometric constructions, and essentials of trigonometry are mostly skills with a bit of foundational knowledge. Making change is mostly a skill. Performing operations with units such as cups, pints and quarts is also mostly a skill. The relative ease with which you learn and then use these skills is your numerical aptitude, which I often call numeracy or simply numbers.

General Skills

Mathematics – Using numbers to communicate, evaluate and solve problems

Reading – Understanding letters, words and sentences

Speaking – Conveying information effectively by talking

Writing – Conveying information effectively through words and sentences using penmanship or keyboarding

Listening – Giving attention, asking questions and discerning important points

Learning - Recognizing, relating, assimilating and applying new information

Driving – Operating a motor vehicle

Computing – Operating a computer

Skill Levels

Working skills might be thought of as job specific applications and levels of general skills. Take driving for example. For many jobs, it's just a matter of getting back and forth from work. For an outside salesperson, driving might be ¾ of their job. For a *UPS* driver operating a larger vehicle, more skill might be required. Driving an 18-wheel tractor-trailer rig, a bit more. A professional *NASCAR* or *Formula One* driver would require a whole different kind of skill at a whole new level. And the underlying natural talents required would be completely different for each level.

Similarly, operating a computer is now a job skill that is increasingly necessary for most jobs. In today's world, basic computer skills, keyboarding and familiarity with software like those found in the *Microsoft Office Suite* are becoming as critical as learning to drive. For one job it might be operating point-of-sale software in a retail environment or doing some simple word processing. Another job might include equipment maintenance, software installation and hooking up a few peripherals like a printer. Another level would be trouble-shooting and repair, then networking, programming and technology design.

*O*NET* Skill List

Skills - <u>Developed</u> capacities. Here is a link to *O"NET* Skills. You can navigate your way to more detailed descriptions: https://www.onetonline.org/find/descriptor/browse/Skills/

The list or table on the next page is based on content in *O*NET*. I think a few of the skills like social perceptiveness edge into the talent-aptitude category, but this can be enhanced with training so it belongs here. Some fall into the soft skill category which we talk about on a following page. It provides a good starter list that can help you brainstorm the skill requirements for any position. The *O*NET* website does connect the skills with a list of nearly 1000 jobs and also provides a solid list of tasks or activities for each of those jobs.

Basic Skills	Complex Problem Solving Skills	Resource Management
Active Learning		Managing Financial Res.
Active Listening		Managing Material Res.
Critical Thinking		Managing Personal Res.
Learning Strategies	**System Skills**	Time Management
Mathematics	Judgment	
Monitoring	Decision Making	**Technical Skills**
Reading Comprehension	Systems Analysis	Equipment Maintenance
Science	Systems Evaluation	Equipment Selection
Speaking		Equipment Installation
Writing		Operation and Control
		Operation Monitoring
Social Skills		Operations Analysis
Coordination		Programming
Instructing		Quality Control Analysis
Negotiation		Repairing
Persuasion		Technology Design
Service Orientation		Trouble Shooting
Social Perceptiveness		

Soft Skills

Increasingly, organizations are more interested in hiring candidates with strong soft skills. These might include things like listening, speaking, conversing, non-verbal communication, conflict resolution, awareness, critical thinking, time management, decision-making, teamwork, leadership and self motivation, creativity and problem solving. Emotional Intelligence books and courses have been popular for the last decade and are related to soft skill awareness and development.

Accessing for Skills

I recommend accessing for skills, often vigorously, but with a view toward the underlying talent. There are some terrific companies that can access for mastery in both hard skills and soft skills. Examples are *eSkill, Skillcheck* and *Total Testing*. When possible, I recommend making up your own tests in the form of a work sample. If you're hiring a welder, have them weld something as part of the interview. If you're hiring a salesperson, have them prepare a presentation and deliver it during the second interview. I don't recommend the popular "Sell Me This Pen" as a work sample demonstration. This work sample is a better indicator of improvisation than selling ability.

Make sure you access all candidates at each screening stage in the same way and make sure an assessment doesn't discriminate against any people group. If in doubt, always run it by an attorney.

Tools – What's The Candidate's "Purple Crayon"

In Deborah Koehn Lloyd's book, *Your Vocational Credo* she writes, "I grew up reading a book called *Harold and the Purple Crayon*. It's about a little boy in foot pajamas with a huge purple crayon. With this crayon he could create any reality he wanted. Sometimes his own imagination carried him away and he found himself in frightful situations. But no problem, he merely drew another scenario and walked out of the scary story and into a safer one. He drew himself into uncharted territory a few times but he always ended up back at home in his cozy little bed." Lloyd believes that her love for the book unlocks awareness for several of her values including creativity, courage and adventure.

Tools can serve as pointers to many of our strengths including our passion, our talents or aptitudes and for the purposes of this chapter, your best skills.

I believe we all have some version of a purple crayon. There is some tool that will work magic when in our possession. The fictional television character known simply as *MacGyver* is well-known for his wizardry with the multi-use *Swiss Army Knife*. With Jimi Hendrix, it was the guitar, a musical instrument that he was known to sleep with. For a writer it might be a pen and yellow pad. For today's writer it might be a *Mac Book Pro* or an app like *Scrivener*. Baseball star Ted Williams was so well acquainted with his bats that he could detect when one came from the factory one ounce heavier or lighter. Edison's tool was his laboratory.

Monkeys, apes, elephants, birds and sea otters are all known to use tools but humans take it to a different level. Some of these animals make tools, but humans are the only creatures known to make meta-tools, that is, tools that make other tools. If scientific dating methods are accurate, it suggest tools date back 2.5 million years.

There are machine tools, musical tools, medical tools, mechanical tools, molding tools, manipulation tools, massive tools and microscopic tools. When Susy and I were on our honeymoon in Kauai, we took a Na Pali Coast cruise. For our captain, the boat was clearly his finely tuned instrument. He expertly backed the boat under a waterfall that seemed dangerously close to sharp rocks, big enough to sink us. That boat was his *Purple Crayon* and he created an adventure for us all!

What's Your Candidate's Purple Crayon?

More Thoughts on Skill

"What I do have are a very particular set of skills; skills I have acquired over a very long career."
~ Bryan played by Liam Neeson, from the movie *Taken*

"Have you ever played a video game that didn't have escalating levels of difficulty? Well, life can feel like play, too, when we purposefully engage in activities that demand we test and develop our skills."
~Brandon Burchard, Author and Speaker

"Somebody once said that in looking for people to hire, you look for three qualities: integrity, intelligence, and energy. And if you don't have the first, the other two will kill you. You think about it; it's true. If you hire somebody without [integrity], you really want them to be dumb and lazy."

~Warren Buffet

Chapter Eight
Staffing for Character

CHARACTER wasn't included in my earliest thinking about strengths. It wasn't because I didn't think character was important. I thought it was critical. But I thought it was critical to happiness. I thought it was critical to a good marriage. I thought it was critical to friendship.

I just didn't see that much of a connection to high performance at work. Oh sure, I understood the importance of honesty for salespeople. But isn't that a given? Then I thought some more...and some more. Examples started coming to mind about careers ruined and performances undermined. And these were not necessarily creepy people. Many were figures I loved and respected from a distance.

There was the popular female vocalist with a powerhouse voice. She was the best in the world.

There was the world-class golfer at the top of his game. He made watching this sport fun again. He seemed destined to break every record on the books.

There was more than one arguably brilliant U.S. President, from both political parties. One was forced to resign and the other was impeached by the House of Representatives.

There were the U.S. House of Representatives members that continued to allow themselves insider information privileges on the stock market.

There were the leaders of a large energy enterprise who misrepresented company financials, eventually bringing down the entire company putting thousands out of work.

There was the pastor, the parish priest and the football coach.

There were the brilliant *Wall Street* bankers whose decisions nearly brought down the United States economy, if not the world economy, causing millions to lose jobs.

There were two car companies that falsified gas mileage records leading their customers to believe they were buying a car that got better gas mileage than it really did.

There was the movie mogul who sexually harassed just about every woman who entered his office.

And there is you and me. Haven't we all stumbled? Haven't we all had a lapse of character?

After reflecting on all that, I knew I had to write this section. For some readers it might be the most important. It might prevent a career-ending move.

When I write about character strengths, I mean moral qualities and decisions. In fact, character strengths are the ones we all can choose.

Consider the following:

Committed – Attendance, Punctuality, Follow Up
Hard Work – Industrious, Diligence, Active, Busy, Initiative
Attitudes – Grateful, Humble, Humor, Cheerful, Fun, Mercy
Respectful – Authority, Honor, Polite, Kind, Fair
Attentive – Fully Present, Anticipation, Awareness
Courageous – Bold, Brave, Grit
Truthful – Sincere, Scrupulous, Trustworthy, Ethical
Excellent – Workmanship, Quality, Presentable, Hygiene
Restrained – Self Control, Discipline, Clean-Sober, Frugal
Safety – Security, Protection

Why is character so important? Great successes always require collaboration. Collaboration requires trust. And trust only flourishes where character qualities are pervasive.

Your character is a huge part of your reputation, what you are known for, and what today is often described as your personal brand.

Character and moral qualities are a crucial part of your *SUCCESSSPATH* package, and they are all a matter of choice!

Core Elements of Personal Integrity

Yale University law professor Steven L. Carter has a three component definition of Personal Integrity that you might find helpful:

1. Discerning what is right and wrong.
2. Acting on what you have discerned, even at personal cost.
3. Saying openly that you are acting on your understanding of right from wrong.

In his book *Executive EQ*, Robert K. Cooper expands on the three, "The first criterion captures the idea of integrity as requiring a degree of moral reflectiveness. The second criterion brings in the ideal of a person of integrity as steadfast, making clear commitments and keeping them at personal risk. The third criterion underscores the fact that a person of integrity is unashamed of doing what he or she believes is true and right and good, and does so openly acting and speaking on behalf of what he or she believes, showing a steadfast devotion to principle, yet being willing to temper this, according to specific circumstances, with compassion."

Cooper continues with one more critical distinction, "One cannot have integrity without being honest, yet one can certainly be honest but have little integrity. By this I mean that a person may be honest without engaging in the hard work of discerning right from wrong in each specific situation, or taking into account the context and feelings and timing involved."

Cooper places Carter's core elements into a kind of formula:

$$D \times (A + V) = 1$$
Discernment x (Action + Voice) = Integrity

That is a lot to think about... Yes? Or Yes!

Accessing for Character

I recommend assessing for character and there are actually indicators on the market for this purpose. But one of the best assessments for character is pretty old school... get references and call them!

The *Google* Code of Conduct – Don't Be Evil
(Borrowed from their website)

"Don't be evil." *Googlers* generally apply those words to how we serve our users. But "Don't be evil" is much more than that. Yes, it's about providing our users unbiased access to information, focusing on their needs and giving them the best products and services that we can. But it's also about doing the right thing more generally – following the law, acting honorably and treating each other with respect.

The *Google* Code of Conduct is one of the ways we put "Don't be evil" into practice. It's built around the recognition that everything we do in connection with our work at *Google* will be, and should be, measured against the highest possible standards of ethical business conduct. We set the bar that high for practical as well as aspirational reasons: Our commitment to the highest standards helps us hire great people, build great products, and attract loyal users. Trust and mutual respect among employees and users are the foundation of our success, and they are something we need to earn every day.

So please do read the Code, and follow both its spirit and letter, always bearing in mind that each of us has a personal responsibility to incorporate, and to encourage other *Googlers* to incorporate, the principles of the Code into our work. And if you have a question or ever think that one of your fellow *Googlers* or the company as a whole may be falling short of our commitment, don't be silent. We want -- and need -- to hear from you.

Who Must Follow Our Code?

We expect all of our employees and Board members to know and follow the Code. Failure to do so can result in disciplinary action, including termination of employment. Moreover, while the Code is specifically written for *Google* employees and Board members, we expect *Google* contractors, consultants and others who may be temporarily assigned to perform work or services for *Google* to follow the Code in connection with their work for us. Failure of a *Google* contractor, consultant or other covered service provider to follow the Code can result in termination of their relationship with *Google*.

I don't think I've ever been a part of an organization where there were no character problems.

Missing the character element always means you will have big messes to clean up. This is sideways and backwards energy that you want to avoid whenever possible.

More Thoughts on Character

"Real character is doing the right thing, knowing that nobody's going to know if you did it or not."
~Oprah Winfrey, Television Personality

"I have a dream that my four little children will one day live in a nation where they will not be judged by the color of their skin, but by the content of their character."
~Martin Luther King, Jr., Civil Rights Leader

"Winning takes talent. To repeat takes character."
~John Wooden, former *UCLA* Basketball Coach

"As you go to work, your top responsibility should be to build trust."
~Robert Eckert, former C.E.O of *Mattel Toys*

"Ask yourself… mercilessly: Do I exude trust? **E-X-U-D-E**. Big word. Do I smack of trust? Think about it. Carefully."
~Tom Peters, Business Author and Speaker

"If you keep to one corner and neglect the myriad aspects of the totality, if you take one thing and discard the rest, then what you attain will be little and what you master will be shallow."

~Lao Tzu

Chapter Nine
Selecting For Other Strength Dimensions

Are there other strengths that should be considered when hiring? I believe there are. At the beginning of this book I shared, "A strength is any resource, internal or external, that can be turned into a marketplace contribution." Here are the dimensions with short explanations to get you started:

Project Phase Preference

Project Phase is a concept introduced by Bobb Biehl, a very smart business consultant. Bobb says that in every organization, and each project within the organization, is always in one of five phases of development: Design Phase – Design/Develop Phase – Develop Phase – Develop/Maintain Phase – Maintain Phase. Bobb believes, and I agree, that each of us has a phase where we thrive. I've simplified his concept based on my background in construction… Architect – Builder – Craftsman - Detailer. If you follow baseball, you know that pitchers can be starters, middle relief or closers. Rarely does one type of pitcher thrive in more than one of the three roles. I've seen this concept work powerfully in my own life in both good ways and bad ways. My dad is a brilliant architect builder who needed to hire people to do punch lists and get the job finished. I'm wired similarly. My wife is a brilliant closer who is compelled to complete everything she starts. I published four books last year largely because she is my editor and has a deep desire to finish.

Anti-Fragility – Advancing in Adversities

Defeats, disappointments, set backs, difficulties, problems and challenges can build wisdom and resilience. Legendary investor Warren Buffett reportedly won't invest in a company where the owner/leader hasn't experienced multiple failures. Lazlo Block says that *Google* has become very intentional about seeking out candidates who have shown resilience and the ability to overcome hardship. But Anti-Fragility takes it a step further. Anti-Fragility is a concept developed by Professor Nassim Nicholas Taleb. He contrasts it with **Resilience** = Recovery - How can I get through this adversity, difficulty...? Resilience is the ability to recover from failure or defeat.

Taleb also contrasts with **Robustness** = Resistance - How can I resist this adversity, difficulty… Robustness is the ability to resist failure, defeat, disappointment. **Anti-Fragile** = Refine/Raise the Bar - How can I get bigger, stronger, better? Anti-fragility is a property of systems that increase in capability, resilience, or robustness as a result of stressors, shocks, volatility, noise, mistakes, faults, attacks, or failures. You want to hire the salesperson who gets better with each rejection. You want to hire the builder who gets better when the last few houses had roofs that sagged.

Tools

Certainly tools are external resources that can be turned into marketplace contributions. At a basic level, this might include appropriate work clothes and transportation to and from work. It might include a work truck with very specific tools, a laptop computer or a computer repair kit. In my case, it includes my *MacBook Pro* and my Career Development Library. Whatever role you're hiring for, I recommend inquiring about the candidate's tools. *O*NET* offers an excellent list of tools to get you started thinking about this category. The list isn't a stand alone but must be accessed through each individual job.

Geography

Certainly your location is a critical and often overlooked component of your STRENGTHSPATH. I was at a strengths workshop recently where speaker/author Steve Witt talked about this. He thinks it's one of the most important considerations of the strengths dimensions that you can choose. I spoke with a Sacramento dentist friend at length about how he factored location into his hiring equation. He found that when he hired candidates that lived on the other side of his sprawling city, they didn't stay long. The commute just ate up too much of their life. Geography fits within my definition of a strength… "Any resource, internal or external that can be used to make a marketplace contribution." Your location can have a lot to do with your ability to contribute. And longevity is part of contribution.

Environment

Some people thrive when they work outdoors. They were made for it. I'm not. I did it for years working in the family construction business and couldn't wait to get inside. This also has to do with your internal temperature needs. It may seem trivial but I've witnessed a lot of workplace conflict over the thermostat.

Other strength issues may come in to play as well. Some people can't concentrate with co-workers close by. Their distraction filter is set differently. Others thrive in a group environment. There is a huge number of articles and online chatter around the Open Office Strategy embraced by *Google* and others. Some are calling it a failure while others are defending it. Different people thrive in different environments. Some tasks and activities are now being described as "Deep Work" where they may require a different atmosphere. You may want to consider helping an associate alter there environment depending on the task at hand. Some of this may have to do with the introvert-extrovert personality dimension briefly described in the chapter on Personality. *O*NET* offers an excellent list of work contexts to get you started thinking about this category:

https://www.onetonline.org/find/descriptor/browse/Work_Context/

Chronotype

Chronotype, also called a biological clock, refers to the behavioral demonstration of underlying circadian rhythms. An individual's chronotype is the biological tendency to sleep at a particular time during a 24-hour cycle. There are "clock genes" that influence metabolism, hormones, body temperature, cognitive function and sleep needs.

Sleep scientists often use lay terminology, larks for morning people and owls for night people. This can be a big deal for some people. I've had friends and family members who operate toward the extremes. Don't think this is something they can control.

I worked for 16 years in an organization that had two different categories of salespeople. One classification went to work at 8 or 9am. The other went to work at 2 or 3pm. Chronotype was an important strength to consider when selecting one position or the other.

Chronotype will drive a candidate's unique Window Of Optimal Performance or their "WOOP" time. Most of us have a 6 to 8 hour window each day where we are most effective. Ideally this should match up with the applicant's job. Don't overlook this component.

I recommend a deeper dive on this topic. Read the book, *The Power of When*, by board certified sleep doctor Michael Breus. Start with his free chronotype assessment which you can find on the internet at thepowerofwhen.com . You will discover if your sleep patterns more closely resemble the lion, the bear, the dolphin or the wolf.

In an interview with Tai Lopez, Dr. Breus tells the story of working with an individual who was about to get fired from her job. She gave the doctor permission to call her boss and her employer bluntly confirmed this. Breus made a small adjustment to her work schedule and it changed everything. The employer was thrilled.

Climate and Seasons

Looking back at my report cards, I always got better grades in the first and fourth quarters of the school year. This was consistent throughout school. I believe I suffer a bit from S.A.D. or Seasonal Affective Disorder and that may have impacted my performance at school.

My wife suffers terribly in the heat. I hate the cold. Both of our dispositions are affected by temperature. We've moved to a climate that generally works for both of us. I worked for two years in an office environment where there was constant vying for control of the thermostat. It affected productivity! Don't assume a candidate can transfer from the coast to the desert without a change in performance.

Pace

Is the candidate the tortoise, the hare or something in between? Are they a sprinter, marathoner or middle distance runner? I often use a metronome as a prop in my workshops because it is such a good illustration of our internal pace. Some of this may be driven by your percentage of fast twitch and slow twitch muscle, which is based on genetics. It is something like torture for a fast-paced person to work in a slow-paced environment or a slow-paced person to work in a fast-paced environment.

The Bible talks about being "Unequally Yoked". It's referring to spiritual values but the concept surely applies to a candidate's pace. You generally will want to partner people with those who match their velocity.

Spiritual Gifts

If you are hiring staff in a faith based non-profit or church, consider this one. I was raised in the church and I've seen these strengths operate powerfully.

Experience

What type of experience did the candidate get in their last job or first job? Most job search candidates undervalue their early work experiences.

Many downplay experience in fast food, retail or jobs that demand physical labor. The candidate was exposed to a lot more than you think.

Imagine two job search candidates with identical experience. Each walks into an interview having worked two years at the same *McDonalds*.

The first candidate is asked about their experience and responds:

"I just flipped burgers, that was pretty much it."

Then the second candidate walks in with identical experience but responds:

"My first job was at *McDonalds*. It was the greatest experience of my life. I still have friends that I made while working there. I'm nowhere near the person I was when I started. I'm grateful for everything they taught me.

I learned how to:

Work with the public
Be responsible
Show up on time
Work under adverse conditions
Handle irate customers
Solve problems and put out fires
Make customers feel comfortable
Work as a team member
Be accountable and work under authority
Implement repeatable systems
Increase my efficiency
Organize, plan and set up
Display ordinary items in an extraordinary way
Process payments
Up-Sell... Do you want fries with that?

The **training was amazing**…It was **great**…It was **wonderful**…I would **do it all over again**…"

The second candidate painted a picture of what they experienced and **how they grew**.

Same experience… who gets the job?

You can learn to understand the strengths in the candidate experiences, and encourage them to give quality responses!

It's probably also worth noting that some companies deliberately hire for inexperience. Supercomputer pioneer Seymore Grey used to hire inexperienced applicants because he believed it brought him more people who "do not usually know what's supposed to be impossible."

School

In his crazy-wonderful book, *Secrets of a Buccaneer-Scholar,* James Marcus Bach talks about *Schoolism* – the belief that schooling is the necessary and exclusive way to get a good education. Bach describes "Education" as the "you" that emerges from the learning you do. Clearly, education can happen in or out of school. That being said, school, including diplomas, report cards, grade point averages, degrees, certificates or certifications can be a strength. Even a record of some coursework can be a positive. Notably, Bach was hired and led a team at *Apple* a few years after dropping out of high school. He has also taught at *Lawrence Livermore National Laboratories* and The *Jet Propulsion Laboratory.*

In his book, *Work Rule!* Lazlo Block talks about *Google's* philosophy of hiring with regard to academic credentials, "The pedigree of your college education matters far less than what you have accomplished. For some roles, it's not important whether you went at all. What matters is what you bring to the company and how you've distinguished yourself." Block also talks about *Google's* philosophy hiring from Ivy League vs. State Schools, "We now prefer to take a bright, hardworking student who graduated from the top of her class at a state school over an average or even above-average Ivy League grad."

Bandwidth

In his book *The Acorn Principle*, Jim Cathcart talks about bandwidth as the capacity to acquire or add capacity. It is the amount of information we can process at one time. This is something akin to RAM inside a computer or a dial up vs. broadband internet access. If you're not up to speed with computer technology, think about the difference between the garden hose you use in the yard and the fire hose used by the local department.

Another way to think about it, is the number of tabs you keep open on your browser. I believe most of our bandwidth is directly related to our synaptic connections and resulting aptitude profile and learning style set up. In other words, we may have tremendous ability to add capacity in one area, yet be limited in another. Think about the bandwidth required in the position you're hiring for.

Thinking Style – 80/18/2

Cathcart also talks about three different styles of thinking: Operational, Strategic and Conceptual. He reports that 80% of the population are Operational Thinkers. They prefer to focus on one thing at a time and deal with each item separately. About 18% are Strategic Thinkers. They process several ideas at once and consider the relative value of each alternative. Conceptuals, who see the big picture and the relationships between everything, compose 2% of the population.

Tribe

A candidate's tribe is the people they hang out with. It is an external resource that can be leveraged into a marketplace contribution. In *The 6 Reasons You'll Get the Job,* Debra Angel MacDougall and Elisabeth Harney Sanders-Park contend that the right associates often add value. Many organizations are looking at online friends. They are asking, "Will the people the candidate knows add value to our organization, or could they be a cause for concern?" Some companies are looking at a candidate's *Klout* score before they hire for certain positions. *Google's* number one method of recruiting has been hiring friends of current employees.

Disabilities

Microsoft and other tech companies are reportedly recruiting employees on the autism spectrum because they are often incredibly gifted in key areas. If you haven't tuned in to *The Good Doctor* or *Scorpion*, you're missing great television as well as an education on how disabilities are sometimes super abilities. Many of the so-called disabilities or limitations are constraints that can be a source of focus. Like the Da Vinci's *"Vitruvian Man"* ideal, the hypothetical *"Vitruvian Brain"* ideal is in rapid decline. A disproportionate number of high level corporate CEO's and entrepreneurs have learning disabilities including dyslexia, It could be argued this so-called "disability" provided them with some advantage. Consider this list of achievers widely believed to be dyslexic:

Charles Schwab - Founder, Discount Brokerage Business
Craig McCaw - Cellular Phone Pioneer
John Reed - Led *Citibank* to the top of the industry
Scott Adams - *Dilbert* Creator
James Carville - Political Consultant
Cher - Singer, Entertainer
Charles "Pete" Conrad Jr. - Astronaut
Erin Brockovich - Activist
Whoopi Goldberg - Actress, Talk Show Host
Dr. Edward Hallowell - Psychiatrist
Bill Hewett - Co-founder, *HP*
Jay Leno - Host of the *Tonight Show*
Nelson Rockefeller - Former Governor of New York
Nolan Ryan - Hall of Fame Baseball Pitcher
Steven Spielberg - Film Maker
Thomas J. Watson Jr. - Former CEO, *IBM*
Henry Winkler - Actor

"Hire and promote first on the basis of integrity, second, motivation, third, capacity, fourth, understanding, fifth, knowledge and last and least, experience."

~Dee Hock

Chapter Ten
Convergence: Selecting for Integration

Google economist Hal Varian says, "We are entering a new period of combinatorial innovation." Eric Schmidt comments, "This occurs when there is great availability of component parts that can be combined or recombined to create new innovations. For example, in the 1800s, the standardization of design of technical devices such as gears, pulleys, chains and cams led to a manufacturing boom. In the 1900s, the gasoline engine led to innovations in automobiles, motorcycles and airplanes. By the 1950s, it was the integrated circuit proliferating in numerous applications."

In a sense we are entering a new phase of hiring innovations with a growing ability to understand multiple components of a perfect match. We are rapidly moving toward having the technology to create much better matches between employees and their jobs. A lot of this innovation will be driven by computerized matching and selection. In the meantime, it's probably not a good idea to consider all the possibilities when it comes to finding a good match.

A great hire is an integrated blend of passion, talent, skill and knowledge. One of the goals of this book is to better explain that integration. To better understand how talent, skill and knowledge enhance each other, consider the following examples:

Music is a passion
Rhythm is talent
Playing drums and dancing are both skills
Musical notation is knowledge

Baseball and Basketball are both passions
Eye-hand coordination is talent
Hitting a baseball and shooting a basketball are both skills
Studying the other team's pitcher or zone defense is acquiring knowledge

Numbers are a passion
Number memory and analytical reasoning are talents
Mathematics and using spreadsheets are skills
Accounting principles and tax law are knowledge

Art is a passion
Spatial vision is talent
Drawing or painting is skill
Art history is knowledge

In his book *Gifted Hands*, brain surgeon Ben Carson talks about this idea of strengths integration. He suggests that surgeons require an "Aptitude Talent" for "Structural Visualization" or being able to see in 3D. But to perform successful brain surgery, you must also acquire a set of skills that come through rigorous training, practice and experience. You need to acquire a very specific kind of knowledge including surgical tools and medical terminology. And you need a detailed understanding of neurological anatomy. None of this skill and knowledge building is probably going to happen without a lot of passion.

Increasingly, the marketplace is becoming very values conscious as leaders realize individual values are the chief components of organizational culture.

Character is critical. Employers are frustrated. So many new employees hired don't understand the importance of regular work attendance and consistently showing up on time.

Dynamic Tensions

Dr. Timothy Butler is the Director of Career Development Programs at *Harvard Business School*. In his book, *Getting Unstuck: A Guide to Discovering Your Next Career Path,* he talks about this idea of "Dynamic Tensions".

As Butler explains it, "One part of the self finds attraction in one direction and another part of the self is drawn to an apparently contradictory direction." Butler believes that some people even become aware of this through images or spontaneous visions. One example might be the sensation of "walking a tightrope". Sometimes these images come up when listening to a popular song that somehow describes or explains the tension or contradiction you're experiencing.

In the *Staffing For Passion* section, I talked about Ed Catmull who had this pull to art, represented by his hero Walt Disney. But he also had this pull toward science, represented by his other hero Albert Einstein. He eventually resolved this conflict by pulling them together in computer animation, a new science based art form which he helped create.

In my workshops, I often give the example of my wife Susy who has two very strong competing values. One part of her is a regimented rule keeper and another part is an independent renegade. She resolved this with two jobs. During the week, rule keeping Susy worked with struggling kids in a continuation high school. Independent Susy was a Rock Star performer in a band every weekend.

Timothy Butler offered up a dynamic tension he calls, "Serving Others" vs. "Being The Star". The example he gave was Dr. Martin Luther King. As Butler explains, part of Dr. King's role, included both his willingness to serve and eventually sacrifice his life. It also included being in the spotlight and becoming something of a star.

In her book, *Mindworks*, trainer Anne Linden explains what *Neuro-Linguistic Programing (NLP)* practitioners call "Parts". Linden says, "By 'parts' I mean aspects or qualities of a person: the efficient part, the stay-at-home part, the nurturing part, the shopper part, the baby, the glamour girl and all the other selves, parts and facets that make up the whole individual, whether or not the person is conscious of them."

Learning to integrate these parts is the artistic side of career development. Like the snowflake, you are a completely unique, one-of-a-kind individual. This is why off-the-rack jobs always need some tailoring, just like a well-made suit of clothes.

Learning to integrate your parts, especially those in tension will require wisdom and some trial and error. It's a little like the story of the wizard and the magic carpet:

A younger wizard wanted a magic carpet just like the old wizard. The old wizard agreed to help and show the young wizard how to weave his own. When the magic carpet was complete, the young wizard was disappointed because it was very plain. The old wizard explained, "The more experiences you have, the wiser you become, the richer and more beautiful your carpet becomes."

Integrating all our parts, including the passions, talents, skills, knowledge and values with their inevitable tensions is like that.

Another relevant story in the passion chapter was under the heading, *Finding The Candidate Mash Up.* The story about the high school kid who stood up in the career direction assembly to explain that he liked walking and he liked turtles. Within minutes the *Roadtrip Nation* staff had him on the phone talking with a "Turtle Walker".

It really is possible to honor all your parts and dynamic tensions. How you can do that may require some time and creativity to pull it all together. You were created to do something absolutely unique and the clues sit before you.

Paradoxical – Complimentary Traits

Paradoxical Traits… AKA Antipodal Traits are desirable candidate traits that appear to be a contradiction. For example, I used to try and hire salespeople who were both aggressive and sensitive. *The Greatest Showman*, P.T. Barnum said, "You must have both caution and boldness to insure success." Many would consider hiring a candidate who is an extrovert to be the better part of wisdom. Introverts after all would resist going out and talking to people. But there is research suggesting that "Ambiverts", a blend of the two, make far better salespeople.

Good to Great author Jim Collins writes about the Leadership Paradox, "The most powerfully transformative executives possess a paradoxical mixture of personal humility and professional will. They are timid and ferocious. Shy and fearless."

Psychologist and *Flow* author Mihaly Csikszentmihalyi identifies ten polar opposite personality traits that extremely creative people hold in "dialectical tension". Adherence to these traits is not merely "wishy-washy", as in being moderately nurturing and moderately competitive, but both fiercely competitive and intensely nurturing; not just a midpoint on a continuum, but an alternating embrace of the extremes. (I would add, sometimes the simultaneous embracing or expression of the extremes.)

1. Energy and Rest
2. Smart and Naïve
3. Disciplined and Playful
4. Fantasy and Realism
5. Extroversion and Introversion
6. Humble and Proud
7. Masculine and Feminine
8. Traditional and Rebellious
9. Passionate and Objective
10. Enjoyment and Suffering

Harrison Assessments is the only hiring oriented testing company that incorporates paradoxical traits in their system. They are worth considering if you need a candidate with the right blend. *Harrison* measures each of 175 traits independently rather than on what they call a "Bi-Polar Scale". For example, *Myers-Briggs* measures four sets of traits against each other. In varying degrees anyone taking that assessment would either be Introverted or Extroverted, Intuitive or Sensing, Thinker or Feeler and

Perceiver or Judge. If *Harrison* were measuring those traits they would measure each independently rather than as polar opposites.

Some examples of the paradoxical or complimentary traits they measure are:

Authoritative – Tendency to take responsibility for decisions
Collaborative – Tendency to allow participation in decision-making

In the *Harrison* world you could have both…
Other examples are:

Self Acceptance – Tendency to like oneself ("I'm OK the way I am.")
Self Improvement – The tendency to develop or better oneself

Organizing – Tendency to maintain order in an environment
Flexibility – Tendency to easily adapt to change

Confidence – Tendency to believe in one's own viewpoint
Open/Reflective – Tendency to reflect on many different viewpoints

Ambitious – Desire to develop one's own financial strength
Benevolence – Desire to help society

Logical – Tendency to use analysis
Intuition – Tendency to use an internal knowing

Fun – Tendency to inject lightheartedness and levity into work
Seriousness – Tendency to inject urgency and resoluteness into work

More Thoughts on Integration

"A winner is someone who recognizes his God-given talents, works his tail off to develop them into skills, and uses these skills to accomplish his goals."
~Larry Bird, former Professional Basketball Player

"We suggest that you take a close look at knowledge, skills, and talents. Learn to distinguish each from the others. Identify your dominant talents and then in a focused way acquire the knowledge and skills to turn them into real strengths."
-Marcus Buckingham, Author and Speaker

"Talent x Investment = Strength"
~Tom Rath, Author and Speaker

"Your talents, passions and conscience together add up to a whole person...If your job requires your skills but not your talents, you will never tap into the genuine and instinctive part of yourself."
~Stephen R. Covey and Jennifer Colosimo, Authors

"When you surround yourself with hugely talented, passionate, dedicated, and genuinely kind people you will succeed in whatever you do."
~Kip Tindell, founder of *The Container Store*

"Be wise as serpents and harmless as doves."
~Jesus Christ

"It's the Genius of Both."

~Jim Collins

"It's surprising how few companies systematically identify their strategically important A positions—and then focus on the A players who should fill them."

~Mark Huselid, Richard Beatty and Brian Becker

Chapter Eleven
"A" Positions:
Identify Mission Critical Roles

According to Logan Loomis, author of *Getting the People Equation Right*, "Mission Critical Jobs are those jobs that are critically important in executing your business strategy. Generally, about 20% of organizational roles are mission critical."

You'll want to extend this philosophy of strengths based hiring throughout every position in your company, but it makes sense to prioritize. I recommend starting with you, the business owner or business unit manager. Are you using your own strengths effectively? Are you doing tasks that would be better performed by another?

Begin making a list of the other mission critical positions in your organization. What are the positions that have the most impact on organizational success? I would argue that customer contact roles always fit in this category but every business is different. The season and size of the business might also impact your decision.

One business consultant, T. Harv Eker argues that there are only three departments in any business:

Sales – Bring in business

Production – Make stuff

Operations – Support sales and production roles while keeping things organized

But each of these departments may have several roles or positions. In some cases it might make sense to select one or two of those positions in each department. Write in your thoughts on mission critical "A" positions here:

Sales

1.

2.

Production

1.

2.

Operations

1.

2.

Self Hiring - You #1 and You #2

Think about your current roles. What are the tasks you perform on an hourly, daily, weekly or monthly basis? Would you hire you?

Bridgewater Investments founder Ray Dalio talks about the You #1 and You #2 Concept. The writing is a little confusing at first but stay with it. I think you'll find it highly valuable. Imagine there are two of you…

You #1 – A Coach = You as the designer and overseer of the plan to achieve your goals.

You #2 – A Player = You as one of the participants in pursuing those goals.

You #1 sees You #2 as one of many resources to get what You#1 wants done.

To be successful, You #1 has to be objective about You #2.

Let's imagine that your goal is to have a winning basketball team. Wouldn't it be silly to put yourself in a position that you don't play well? If you did, you wouldn't get what you want. Whatever your goals are, achieving them works the same way.

If You #1 sees that You #2 is not capable of doing something, it is only sensible for You #1 to have someone else do it. In other words, You #1 should look down at You #2 and all the other resources at You #1's disposal and create a "machine" to achieve You #1's goals.

Remember that You #1 doesn't necessarily need to do anything other than design and manage the machine to get what You #1 wants. If You #1 finds that You #2 can't do something well, fire You #2 and get a good replacement!

You #1 shouldn't be upset that You #2 is bad at that. You #2 should be happy because You #1 has improved You #1's chances of getting what You #1 wants. If You #1 is disappointed because You #2 can't be the best person to do everything, You #1 is terribly naive because nobody can do everything well.

The biggest mistake most people make is to not see themselves and others objectively. If they could just get around this, they could live up to their potential.

In the early days of professional sports, player coaches were actually fairly common. The most recent example was Bill Russell, who for a time both played and coached the *Boston Celtics* basketball team

Business coach Marshall Goldsmith talks about a similar concept he calls the "Planner-Doer". Goldsmith shares, "We display **two discreet personas I call 'planner' and 'doer'.** The planner who wakes up in the morning with clear plans for the day is not the same person later in the day who has to execute those plans…. Basic tools such as anticipating, avoiding, and adjusting to risky environments are a good place to start correcting this conflict between planner and doer in us."

"Once you know the strengths profile of someone who is great at a role, the person specification part of the job description must reflect that. In essence that means that the ideal person is described in terms of their strengths and other essential requirements but behavioral competencies are usually entirely replaced by the strengths profile."

~Sally Bibb

Chapter Twelve
The "A" Candidate Profile

Now, select one mission critical role and write the position name in the margin. Do you really know what factors cause people to succeed in that given role? I would argue, not very often. Most of us proceed based on stereotypical ideas and faulty assumptions. Consider writing a computer code. Jim Benson offers the following example in his book, *Personal Kanban*:

"Take A-List coders. Characterized by the (alleged) quality of the code they write, the (alleged) speed at which they work, and their (alleged) ability to deliver exactly what their bosses ask for, A-List coders are the holy grail of software design. Rumors of their miraculous powers notwithstanding, A-List is merely a convenient and unscientific distinction. There is no certification or test to become an A-List coder. In spite of this, there seems to be a legitimate group of coders who routinely outperform others in stressful situations."

Ideal Candidate Profile

You don't have the time or the resources to evaluate every applicant who strolls in your office. To guide your selection process, you will benefit from developing a profile of your "ideal" candidate. You may never find your ideal, but you will establish a basic framework that outlines the person you are looking for.

Ideal Candidate Profiling involves paying careful attention to the specific activities involved in successfully doing a job. Most all jobs are really "mosaics" of several tasks, often 60, 100 or more. For example, accounting is not a single activity.

Make sure to list the **Achievements** or Key Results or Outcomes of the position. These Key Results should become the main drivers of the person you're looking for.

Achievement List – Key Results or Outcomes (Accounting Example)
Identify insurance needs and set up coverage for 9 divisions
Clean up receivables bringing in 80% of behind accounts
Establish an accounting system managing over $10M fund

Then, make a detailed **Activity List**.

Activities – Tasks (Accounting Example)
Operate _____ accounting software to record & analyze information
Check financial documents for correct entry, accuracy, and proper codes
Classify, record, and summarize numerical and financial data
Compile and keep financial records
Debit, credit, and total accounts on spreadsheets and databases
Operate 10-key to produce calculations and documents
Receive, record, and bank cash, checks, and vouchers
Comply with federal, state, and company regulations
Compile statistical, financial, accounting or auditing reports and tables
Record receipts, expenditures, payables, receivables, profits & losses
Code records according to company procedures
Reconcile and report discrepancies found in documents

KSAPs

Then build a list of **KSAPs**. This list is used to distinguish the "qualified candidates" from the "unqualified candidates" for a position. KSAPs is an acronym for **K**nowledge, **S**kills, **A**ptitudes, **P**assion. Specific KSAPs are needed in performing certain jobs. Individual KSAPs may be demonstrated through qualifying work experience and education/training. I also recommend adding some type of pre-interview assignment and an interview work sample to the process. KSAPs are defined as:

Knowledge - An organized body of information and facts required to perform a job, activity or task. This is your area of expertise. This may include knowledge of terminology, concepts, rules and regulations.

Knowledge (Accounting Example)
Economics and Accounting — Knowledge of economic and accounting principles and practices, the financial markets, banking and the analysis and reporting of financial data.
Mathematics — Knowledge of arithmetic, algebra, geometry, calculus, statistics, and their applications.
Clerical — Knowledge of administrative and clerical procedures and systems such as word processing, managing files and records, stenography and transcription, designing forms, and other office procedures and terminology.
Administration and Management — Knowledge of business and management principles involved in strategic planning, resource allocation, leadership technique, and coordination of people and resources.
Law and Government — Knowledge of laws, legal codes, court procedures, precedents, government regulations, executive orders, agency rules, and the democratic political process.

Skills - The proficiency with steps, methods, procedures and sequences you have learned that apply to the successful completion of job tasks and activities. It may also include proficiency with specific tools or technology. When hiring for welding positions, my dad had a kit close by and requested that the candidate weld something.

General Skills (Accounting Example)
Active Listening — Give full attention to what other people are saying, take time to understand the points being made, ask questions as appropriate, and not interrupt at inappropriate times.
Mathematics — Use mathematics to solve problems.
Critical Thinking — Use logic to identify alternative solutions, conclusions or approaches.
Judgment/Decision Making — Consider the relative costs and benefits of potential actions.

97

Complex Problem Solving — Identify complex problems and evaluate options and solutions.
Monitoring — Assess performances to make improvements or take corrective action.
System Analysis — Evaluate system change conditions and operational impact.

Specific Skills (Accounting Example)
Asset Cost Accounting
Payables & Receivables
Payroll
Purchase Orders
Revenue Recognition
General Ledger Analysis
Balance Sheets

Specific Tools (Accounting Example)
QuickBooks
Peachtree
Excel

Aptitudes - The natural inclination or talent to perform an activity or task is foundational to this hiring strategy. You want to hire people who perform the required tasks easily.

Aptitudes (Accounting Example)
Mathematical Reasoning — The ability to choose the right math formulas to solve a problem.
Number Facility — The ability to add, subtract, multiply, or divide quickly and correctly.
Deductive Reasoning — The ability to apply general rules to problems and produce answers.
Near Vision — The ability to see details at close range (within a few feet of the observer).
Inductive Reasoning — The ability to combine pieces of information to form general rules or conclusions (includes finding a relationship among seemingly unrelated events).
Problem Sensitivity — The ability to tell when something is wrong or is likely to go wrong. It does not involve solving the problem, only recognizing there is a problem.
Information Ordering — The ability to arrange things or actions in a certain order or pattern according to a specific rule or set of rules (e.g., patterns of numbers, letters, words, pictures, mathematical operations).
Category Flexibility — The ability to generate or use different sets of rules for combining or grouping things in different ways.
Selective Attention — The ability to concentrate on a task over a period of time without being distracted.
Perceptual Speed — The ability to quickly and accurately compare similarities and differences among sets of letters, numbers, objects, pictures, or patterns.
Flexibility of Closure — The ability to identify or detect a known pattern (a figure, object, word, or sound) that is hidden in other distracting material.

Passion - The love of a job activity or task as well as the subject matter involved. Hire someone who is fascinated by the area of work they are being hired for.

Passion (Accounting Example)
A Deeply Embedded Life Interest in **Quantitative Analysis:**
The quantitative analysis core function represents an interest in solving problems through mathematical analysis. A person who is drawn to the number side of work. An interest in what the balance sheet reveals, whether the assumptions built into the business plan or sales forecasts are accurate, how the spreadsheet represents the market analysis. This is a person who is attracted to work where high-quality quantitative analysis lies at the heart of organizational success. Outside of work this individual engages in problem solving that requires mathematical skill. This person is drawn to investments and money management. They may be the one others turn to for financial advice. Work interests may include information manager, financial analyst, personal financial advisor, economist, chief financial officer, investment banker, accountant, investment manager, stockbroker, credit manager, statistician, theoretical physicist, logistical planner.

The difference between a Strengths Oriented Selection process and Competency Oriented Selection process has much to do with the priorities around these four categories. The Competency Oriented process is focused primarily on Skills and Knowledge, often using stated education and experience as the key qualifiers. The Strengths Oriented Selection process includes these components but adds a much stronger emphasis on the candidate's underlying Passion and Aptitude. Again, Strengths Oriented Selection isn't just interested in whether or not an applicant can do a job, it is very interested in how much the candidate wants to do it and how easily, how quickly and how well they perform the required tasks and activities. Strengths Oriented Selection is also concerned with how quickly and easily the applicant might learn to perform related tasks and activities as technologies shift in the future.

"Your job ads push away talent when they say, 'You must have an MBA, significant experience with these three tools, and at least two of these four certifications.' That's the worst possible way to find talented people. Your job ad should say, 'Write three paragraphs that tell me why this is exactly the job you should be doing.' How hard is that? It requires someone thoughtful and mature to read the responses. Recruiting is your company's most important function. Can you devote just enough attention to it to substitute bulk keyword searching with human judgment and discretion? If you can't, do you have any claim to a leadership culture at all?"

-Liz Ryan, from *Business Week*

Chapter Thirteen
Attraction Advertising

Advertised Position Names

Jobs are frequently advertised <u>under a wide variety of position names</u>. For example, consider positions that are accounting or money related:

Accountant
Bookkeeper
Tax Preparation Specialist
Payable Clerk
Receivable Clerk
Payroll Clerk
Accounts Clerk
Budget Analyst
Treasurer
Controller
Chief Financial Officer
Bank Teller
IRS Examiner
Accounting Software Sales

Every profession goes by more than one name. You will want to develop a list of what different organizations call the role or position you are hiring for and get a sense of what the most common names are. This may be completely different than your organization's in-house name! That issue alone could be costing you many qualified candidates.

To get started, go to www.onetonline.org. In the Occupation Quick Search, in the upper right hand corner, type in the name of the profession you're hiring for. You will come to a page of positions that are loosely in that field. Click on the one that is most similar to your target. This will bring you to a page that displays a sample of reported job titles. This is a good starting list. When you use a job board, you will want to use as many of the different job names as possible.

Writing Ads That Attract... And Repel

The best advice I've seen on writing an employment ad comes from advertising expert Roy H. Williams. I devour every book he writes and review them regularly. Roy offers three rules for writing employment ads:

"**Rule 1: The ad should be about the employee, not the job.** Right now, someone is perusing employment postings for the position you hope to fill. If only you could figure out how to motivate them. Like you and me, this person has aspirations, interests, and strengths. So how do you make your ad more compelling than the others? What is the magic ingredient that will make your ad irresistible? You need only describe the person you hope to find! Speak to their aspirations, interests and strengths. Your dream employee will probably not know of your business. They will not recognize the job you detail. You can, however, be confident that they will recognize themselves when that is who you describe. They will see themselves in the words you choose, the actions you prescribe, and the admirable traits you require. 'That's me!' they will cry. 'What a perfect fit!'

Rule 2: Questions are the answer. There's nothing more irresistible than a question. Have you ever tried to ignore one? Have you ever read a question that was aimed at you and completely escaped thinking about the answer? I doubt it. If, in your job posting, you are willing to ask for exactly what you want, you will probably get it. By raising the bar and challenging a prospect to answer your questions, you will weed out the losers and energize the winners. When your future employee reads a description of themselves in your ad, they will feel like they're looking into a mirror.

'Wow!' they will think. 'What serendipity! This is the position I was born to fill.'

    Rule 3: You get what you pay for. You already know that the cheapest option is rarely the best. This is certainly true with job postings. Stingy, short, choppy ads communicate a lack of respect for the position. They give the impression you really don't care. They effectively say, 'Take it or leave it.' Job postings are no different than ads that sell a product or service. If you want a job posting to be boring, write about the job. If you want it to work miracles, write about the person you hope to find and don't be stingy with your words."

    Roy Williams offers the perfect summary of the strengths based employment advertising advice and models offered by both *Gallup* and *The Marcus Buckingham Company*. Here is a model strengths oriented ad starter for an accountant:

Accountant
Do you "geek out" over balance sheets?
Are you a number cruncher who wants to make a positive impact on the bottom line?
Are you an analytical thinker?
Do you enjoy finding strategies to be more efficient and to maximize financial resources?
Are you able to see more than just numbers when viewing data?
Do you see patterns, relationships, and opportunities?
Are you precise, and can you create systems that help ensure accuracy?
Are your records beautifully organized and accurate in every detail?

Eligibility Qualifications
Two to five years of relevant accounting experience.
CPA or other designation.
Bachelor's degree in accounting, finance, or a related area — are preferred.
Must be proficient in *Microsoft® Excel®*.

Job Advertisement Builder

Common Job Titles

Suitability – Traits in Question Form
Passion (Intense Interest, Enjoyable Work):
Talents (Knack, Flair, Natural Ability, Aptitudes):
Personality (Work Style, Temperament):
Values/Culture (Ideals, Motivations, Priorities):

Eligibility Requirements
Knowledge Required:
Skills Required:
Tools & Tech Required:
Education Required:
Experience Required:
Lic/Training Required:

Job Summary
Tasks:
Activities:

Job Basics
Company Name (This may be moved toward the top if your company is well-known):
Job Title:
Job Number/ID:
City:
County:
Zip Code:
Salary:
Benefits:

How To Apply
Applicant Tracking Link:
Email Link:
Phone Number?
Contact Name?

"Corporate job sites are awful. They are difficult to search, filled with generic job descriptions that don't tell you anything about what the job really is or what the team you'll be part of is like, and provide no feedback on whether you'd be good for a role or not."

~Lazlo Block

Chapter Fourteen
Applicant Journey

Strengths Oriented Staffing specialists need to start looking at candidates as customers as well. For candidates and applicants, the application process is very similar to that of purchasing a product. Similar thought processes and time investments are required. It's estimated that on average, a job seeker spends 45 minutes filling out an application or *buying into the company*. I've actually spent 4-5 hours completing assessments. I've also spent multiple days on the entire application process plus up to 5 or 6 interviews. If you're hoping to attract top candidates who are currently employed, you will lose many of them asking them to jump through this many hoops.

I recommend filling out your own application and timing the whole process. Keep in mind that the best applicants are already employed and probably not even looking for a job.

When an applicant is looking and applying for jobs, they are buying into your brand, environment, atmosphere and culture. The communication of your culture should be accurate and consistent. Keeping an applicant interested in your company is critical throughout the selection process. Having a high application abandonment rate is a time waster for both you and the candidate. Keep an eye on this metric and address it in your recruitment strategy. If your hiring or selection process is difficult, that word spreads fast. You will miss out on opportunities to hire great candidates down the road because they have heard about the complicated tedious process from friends. This may be understandable in times of high unemployment when there is an over supply of good applicants. But often hiring managers and human resource directors may forget to shift their strategy when the unemployment rate is very low.

Further, the applicant may actually be a potential customer for your company's product or service. You could be driving away customers by how you treat your applicants.

Put together a multistep "Applicant Journey" considering all the touch-points in the hiring process. Think about each step deeply from the candidate's perspective. **Think like** *Disney* **or** *Pixar*. **Make a storyboard of the candidate journey including each critical touch point. A sample is on the next page. If you're struggling to get the best people, think of each connection as a place to improve.**

The strengths oriented staffing process is designed to be candidate friendly from beginning to end. Even those candidates who are not selected should leave the process understanding why and more importantly with a better understanding of their own strengths. Some companies actually do workshops with the candidates after the hiring process is over. This is an opportunity for the company to get candidate feedback and help applicants learn about places they might fit in the future.

Ask candidates about their overall experience with the interview process and how it compares to other interviews they've had. It's kind of like an exit interview for people you don't hire.

Applicant Journey Storyboard

1. Employee Referral	2. Job Posting	3. Company Website
4. Application	5. Application Acknowledgement	6. Assignment
7. Assessment	8. Phone Screen	9. Interview Environment
10. Audition-Interview	11. Interview Follow-Up	12. Interview Workshop

"It is a fine thing to have ability, but the ability to discover ability in others is the true test."

~Elbert Hubbard

Chapter Fifteen
Applications

The application form on the following pages is a very non-traditional example. The focus is on what the applicant enjoys doing and wants to do in the future rather than what they've done in the past. You may need to incorporate traditional application elements but I encourage you to resist the urge!

I've listed many more questions than I would ever expect you to use on the application form you build. Try to get the form down to one or two pages and something that can be filled out in 20 minutes. Use a similar form as an outline for your brief phone screen and your job interview questions. The application and the interview should be connected.

Fill out an application yourself. Have others fill it out. Refine the application until it's fun! Heresy... Yes, I know... but try it. Think about the incongruence of trying to sell a candidate on how great your company is and such a wonderful place to work... Yes... we know our job application is a bit nasty... but it really is a great place to work.

For comparison, go apply at several other companies. Find some models of companies where the process is easy and even fun. And fill out one or two that are traditional, maybe even a bit difficult. Walk in the applicant's shoes for a bit.

Strengths Oriented Application

We want to hire candidates who are interested in self-discovery and doing work they are both passionate about and talented for. Qualified applicants receive equal consideration. No question is asked for the purpose of securing information to discriminate against any applicant due to race, creed, color, national origin, religion, age, sex, handicap, veteran status, marital status, sexual orientation, or any other characteristic protected by law. We are an equal opportunity employer.

Personal Information

Today's Date _____

SSN ____-___-_____

Last Name _____ First Name _____ Middle _____

Address _____ City _____ State ___ Zip _____

Phone _____ Work _____ Alt _____

Dream Job
Position you'd love to work toward? _____ How long has this been a dream? _____

What would you love to earn? _____

Education
What were your favorite classes in elementary school?

What were your favorite classes in high school?

What were your favorite classes in college or other career training?

What are the subjects you learned quickly and easily?

Experience – Work History
On your very best day at work – the day you came home and thought you had the very best job in the world – what did you do that day? (*Facebook* Question)

What kind of problems were you good at solving?

How were customers and colleagues lives better when they crossed your path?

What are you proud of contributing?

What was your favorite job ever and why? Favorite Project? Favorite Assignment? Favorite Task?

Passions & Intense Interests
What do you do in your spare time?

What is the single focus and activity that would keep you absolutely fascinated and motivated for the rest of your life? (The *Dan Sullivan* Question)

In order to be optimal, the one thing my workday must have is _____
(The answer is not coffee! It should be a work activity or task)

Talents

What's your superpower?

What's your secret weapon?

What are you insanely great at?

Identify your *"Factory Settings"*. What did you love doing between the ages of 5 and14? What were you good at?

What activities and tasks do you have an instinctive feel for? What's your version of a "green thumb"?

What are your "Made-For-This-Moments"? What are the times or activities where you felt like you were made to do that?

What activities do you find *impossible* not to get involved with? What can't you <u>not</u> do?

Where or when are you the most creative? What are the situations where you come up with ideas?

When do you easily go off script and improvise?

What do you see or notice that other people don't?

What is your genius? How are you smart?

Which of your talents aren't getting used?

Awesome-Average-Awful – On the categories below - In the first section, write down work activities that make you feel awesome. In the second section average. In the third section, write work activities that make you feel awful.

Awesome	Average	Awful

Personality
What emoji best describes you? (Draw the face)

What symbol or symbols would you use to describe yourself?
! ?@ # $ & < > / = + - Why?

How would you describe yourself? List 3-5 traits

Do you ponder or socialize?

Do you prefer to use your intuition or one of the 5 senses?

Do you like structure or making it up as you go?

Do you prefer to go solo or with a partner?

What are your quirks?

Values & Ideals
An ideal world/work/workplace would have more…?

What's important to you in a company or organization?

How would you describe your philosophy?

What are the wrongs in the world that must be set right? What makes you angry?

What traditional belief would you most like to challenge?

What is difficult for you to tolerate?

What day-to-day irritations do you experience?

Learning Style
How do you learn? Listening? Reading? Doing? Writing? Talking? Drawing? Thinking?
Imagine that you have received some new piece of equipment that you have never used
before – a bicycle – a snowboard – a computer… How would you go about learning
to use the equipment? Would you open the owner's manual and read it cover to cover?
Would you just start trying stuff learning by trial and error? Would you call a friend and ask for
advice? Would you enroll in a class?

Knowledge
What kind of information just seems to jump in your head?

What subjects are you an expert in?

Who are your current teachers, trainers or coaches?

If you had to teach a subject, what would it be?

Where is your vocabulary/terminology strongest?

What is your biggest area of ignorance?

What subjects are you most curious about?

Skills

If your life depended on naming a skill at which you're in the top 1% of the world, what would it be?

What skill would you enjoy increasing 25% in the next year?

Where are you regularly trying to grow and get better?

If there was one thing you'd start doing differently tomorrow to unleash more of your potential, what would it be?

What is your "Magic Tool", the tool that allows you to work magic?

Character Qualities

Where are you the best at keeping your commitments?

When do you not keep your commitments?

What internal direction or intuition have you ignored?

What irritating thing do you do without thinking?

Miscellaneous

What time of day are you most effective? Are you a night owl or a morning dove?

Imagine you extended your life 10 years or even for eternity. What three activities would you choose to incorporate daily?

What is your vision of paradise on earth? What about that vision really captivates you?

What's the best thing about you that very few people know?

Write/Share a S.T.A.R. Story Paragraph

S.T.A.R. stands for **S**trength, **T**arget, **A**ction, **R**esult.

Write a short Success Story about yourself from work, school, sports, a hobby or volunteer activity. Briefly, with a sentence for each of the four points, list:

The **S**trength you used

The **T**arget you defined

The **A**ction you took

The **R**esult you achieved

Strengths Oriented Application – Reflection

At the beginning of this chapter I made the suggestion that you walk in the shoes of an applicant. Did you fill out a few applications from other organizations? Which application would you prefer to fill out - the traditional application or the Strengths Oriented Application?

Which application would help the applicant learn more about themselves and the work they really are a good fit for?

Which application would tell you more about the candidates real potential?

Which application would leave the candidate feeling good about themselves and your company?

Which application would leave the applicant feeling like your company really cared about them as a person?

Which application would they tell their friends and relatives about?

Which application would encourage them to have their son and daughter apply for?

Show Up Ratio

Which application would engage curiosity and encourage a higher show up rate for the initial interview? During my eight year tenure as a hiring manager up and down the West Coast I endured an abysmal show up rate. I would routinely try to schedule 10 candidates spaced throughout the day. My show up rate averaged around 20% or two out of ten candidates showing up. This was consistent from San Diego to Seattle and many smaller communities in between.

I really believe that having the candidate fill out a Strengths Oriented Application in advance and return it by email, would have dramatically improved my appointment to show-up ratio.

Appreciative Application Response

Hello Dale!

We are so happy to hear from you and cannot wait to learn more about your strengths, passions, and special skills!

We'll be reviewing your resume and cover letter. Should your superpowers align with what we need in this role -- you better believe you'll be hearing from us.

We wish we could talk to every single applicant, regardless of fit, because nothing makes us happier than learning about the unique gifts you bring to the world! Sadly, due to the large number of applicants we get daily, we can't do that.

So if you don't hear back from us, it's not because you're not incredibly amazing. **You are.** It's because there just happened to be another smashing candidate that really stood out as the perfect fit for this special role.

We hope you get to do what you love everyday. And we hope it's with us. Please stay connected.

VP, People + Culture

Is that not a super classy follow up to a submitted resume and application package? You want to leave people feeling good about your application and hiring process. If you don't hire them immediately, you may have a perfect fit down the road. Or an acquaintance may be the perfect fit. Make people feel good regardless of how well they fit your current needs!

Assignments

Assignments are a great way to identify strengths in a candidate. *Google* co-founder, Sergey Brin was looking for an executive with a particular skill set. He was considering lawyers and gave the following assignment: Write a contract that is well-done, comprehensive and funny. One lawyer delivered an agreement that was titled: Contract 666. The details suggested that Brin had sold his soul to the devil in exchange for one dollar and other considerations.

Van Halen was a top rock band that toured for many years. They had a very detailed contract that contained a "Brown *M&M*" clause. Band member David Lee Roth explained that the clause also contained a provision stating that the promoter would forfeit all pay if this clause was ignored.

What was the big deal? Was *Van Halen* just being difficult? Roth explained the rationale behind the contract provision. To summarize, the clause was in place to check the detail orientation and the local stage set up crew. If the band found brown *M&M's* back stage this was a tip off that the promoter had either not read the agreement or not paid attention to details. Why was that important? It was a safety issue. *Van Halen* toured with a set of 850 lights. This required special stage trusses and electrical considerations. Lighting could collapse and electrical system overloads could occur. The band was confident that if the brown *M&M* issue was handled properly, the safety issues would be handled as well. If the band showed up and found brown *M&M's* back stage, they immediately checked every detail of the staging. What does this have to do with staffing and selection? A lot!!!

Creative assignments can help you understand a candidate's:

Sense of Humor
Flexibility
Imagination
Improvisation Ability
Problem Solving

Creative assignments may also help understand an applicant's:

Sense of Detail
Ability to Follow Directions
Work as Part of a Team

The following are two examples:

Assignments Within A Job Description

You will be a front-line representative, in charge of delivering exceptional customer service to clients. You will take inbound calls, explain how the program works, help potential customers sign up, review account status, provide guidance on product features, re-enforce product value to retain current customers and ensure customer satisfaction.

We are looking for out-going people who are super-friendly and have great attitudes!

The main responsibility of the Customer Service Representative is to provide prompt, friendly, and accurate support for cardholders. This role requires the ability to resolve customer inquiries, escalate as needed, follow up with customers, and multitask on related activities. You will be the face and voice of this company. You will need to listen carefully to what the customer is saying while maintaining a super-friendly, polite and helpful attitude.

We are a growing company and this is a growth opportunity for the right candidate. **So that I know you read this, please start the first line of your cover letter with the sum of the numbers five and two. Your email will not reach us if you don't follow this exact instruction**. (**The company that wrote this job description did not underline or place the request in bold.** The candidate that I was coaching had not read the request and was about to send off her application cover letter without the required information.)

Pre-Interview Assignment
To apply, please send the following:
Resume
Cover Letter
A short story that demonstrates that you are super-friendly.

Case-Studies

Case-studies are another form of assignment that can be used prior to an interview, during an interview, in-between a sequence of interviews and post-interview. Recruiting expert Lou Adler talks about one form of this option that he calls a "Take-Home Project".

Lou writes, "The take-home project is something the candidate does outside of the interview that's discussed at a subsequent meeting. Topics for this can include reviewing reports, solving real job-related problems, evaluating new products, assessing tactical or strategic plans, and providing consulting advice on a mini-project. The take-home project is effective because the candidate is required to do real work, not just talk about it."

Lou believes that the take-home project reveals real passion or motivation and desire. Candidates won't spend much time preparing if they're not truly interested in the job.

One computer company down the street from me pays candidates to work a four-hour shift before offering them a position.

When running a staffing company that outsourced a lot of welders, my father kept a welding kit in the office. He instructed each candidate to "Weld Something".

"Because of the biases with which we are wired, our self-assessments and our assessments of others tend to be highly inaccurate. Psychometric assessments are much more reliable. They are important in helping understand how people think during the hiring process and throughout employment."

~Ray Dalio

Chapter Sixteen
Assessments

In an *Inc. Magazine* interview, Tony Robbins talks about how he uses assessments as part of the hiring process, "We give **our candidates** a personality test that, among other things, answers the question: What is the person's nature? Everyone is a mix of, I'll use the shorthand, heart, hands, and head. Heart is your level of empathy. If someone who is completely leading with his heart is in a business meeting and we start talking about firing someone, his first focus is going to be, 'Oh, what will that do to this person?' A person who is more hands-driven is more pragmatic. For her, it's like, 'How do we get this done?' And she might still have a big heart, but it's really important to her that we don't just go in circles talking about %#*^. A head person is systemic, so a systemic person wants to go, 'Oh, slow everything down.' So the pragmatic person makes the systemic person crazy, the systemic person makes the pragmatic person want to kill him, and the heart-driven person is a sweetheart who seems to be off in left field. We all have all three of these qualities, and the test measures where they fall on a scale of zero to 10. We then give that **raw data** to the potential employee and say, 'Circle everything you disagree with and tell us why.' It gives us a jumping-off point, because I don't want to just be sold and I don't wanna sell you on us. I want to have a sustainable relationship." Robbins has historically used a

D.I.S.C. assessment from *Innermetrix*. This is a terrific version of *D.I.S.C.* and I've used it myself for many years.

Dave Ramsey uses this *D.I.S.C.* as well. Each employee has their *D.I.S.C.* profile summary on their office door. This is such a great way to keep the information top of mind and make it useful on an ongoing basis.

Ray Dalio at *Bridgewater Associates*, one of the world's most successful investment firms is a huge fan of the *Myers-Briggs* assessment.

Why Use Hiring Assessments?

When conducted correctly, **the assessment is objective, as opposed to subjective**. By using objective assessment, the emotional response is eliminated, so the attitude of the person making the selection or determining a person's suitability is not influenced by their personal views.

Assessments "tee-up" or start discussions about job fit, specifically those abilities that increase the likelihood of success in a particular position.

Assessments help move beyond issues of candidate eligibility and into issues of candidate suitability for a particular role.

Assessments can help identify the unique abilities of those already performing the job at a high level therefore creating the basis for ability benchmarks.

Assessments can help in the creation of a more accurate job description.

Assessments can narrow a hiring pool down to the candidates most likely to succeed.

Assessments can help create structured ability interview questions and begin interview conversations with a candidate about suitability and job fit.

Assessments can be a fair tie-breaker when two or more candidates appear approximately equal.

When used properly, assessments, because of their anonymous nature can help insure legality, uniformity and fairness while guarding against adversely impacting any group.

Assessments can improve the candidate's initial impression about **the professionalism of the company**. It has been estimated that **3 out of 10 individuals will turn down a job offer.** Assessments can help sell the candidate on the company.

Some may think that assessments are a misguided modern invention. Actually, the Chinese are believed to have invented career assessment for hiring purposes over 4000 years ago. The first may have been civil service examinations that were designed to select all of the emperor's officials. Some of the work sample tests were designed to identify proficiency in subjects as far ranging as arithmetic, archery, music, writing and even ceremonial skills. Candidates were also often assessed for their ability to understand the Confucian classics, memorization, as well as their ability to compose essays and poems. Specific procedures were established, with independent assessments that included at least two assessors and a fairly rigorous standardization of test conditions. In some respects, it was similar to what many top companies do today.

The idea of traits and factors in matching people to jobs may have first popped up in the U.S. in the early 1900s. It probably existed before that, but Frank Parsons gets credit for his book, *Choosing a Vocation*, published by *Houghton Mifflin* in 1909. Many of today's career counselors still venerate Parsons as something of a founder or an early influence. *Western Electric's* John Mills came up with an assessment that he used informally in interviews. It's believed that he first began using the idea in 1918, but it was formally written up in 1921. Mills, who believed that a career should be defined as "the expression of one's own personality, working through some medium" would put four categories on separate cards. The categories were:

1. Ideas
2. People
3. Things
4. $ Symbols or Economic Symbols

Mills would ask each applicant in an interview to simply arrange each of the four cards in order of decreasing interest. This basic idea is still used by many career counselors today.

Serious research on talent, temperament and the natural inclinations of everyday people, was also introduced in the writings of psychiatrist Carl Jung. Jung began piggybacking on the thinking of classical philosophers like Hippocrates and Galen. Over a two millennia earlier, they had hypothesized about Four Human Temperaments or Personality Styles they were observing. Departing from the Freudian inclination to study darker behavioral aberrations, Jung became fascinated with "Typological" behavior or normal people. Katharine Cook Briggs and her daughter, Isabelle Briggs Meyers, built on Jung's work developing what we know today as the *Myers-Briggs Temperament Assessment*.

In the 1920's, a contemporary of Jung, psychiatrist William Marston, wrote *The Emotions of Normal People*. Marston's writing later developed into early versions of what we now call the DISC assessment. Early versions of both the *Myers-Briggs* assessment and the *DISC* assessment were used by the *U.S. Army*. In the era leading up to World War II, they were implemented as a method of placing soldiers in work that fit them. After the war ended, the assessments found their way into the business world, again helping with job placement. Both instruments are still being refined for business use today by a variety of companies with both psychological and industrial backgrounds. (As a side-note, William Marston was the developer of both the polygraph or lie-detector machine, as well as the comic book and film character Wonder Woman)

While Jung, Marston, and the *Myers-Briggs* team were working on temperaments, personality and typology, something else was going on with researchers in a *General Electric* plant found in Lynn, Massachusetts.

In 1922, Johnson O'Conner headed the engineering department at that plant. O'Conner was a young, brilliant, philosophy graduate from *Harvard University* who worked as an assistant to Percival Lowell in astronomical-mathematical research. At *G.E.* he worked under F.P. Fox who was actually the founder of the Lynn, Massachusetts plant.

Like most companies, Cox and O'Conner were interested in reducing costs and increasing efficiencies of the plant workers. The pair hit on a concept that is foundational to career assessment philosophy. It seemed to them that if people did work that was both natural and right to them, not only would this compatibility (rightness) boost efficiency, but it would make them take a greater interest in their jobs. The jobs themselves would have to be examined and work samples (tests) for each would have to be used.

Legal Issues

Today, literally hundreds of different assessments are in use by hiring managers and human resource departments. When using assessments as a selection instrument, employers must be sure there is no "adverse impact" on any one group. Not all assessments are suitable for use as pre-employment assessments. Specifically, psychological assessments that were designed for clinical or diagnostic use, should not be used.

The use of clinically inclined instruments would also violate the *Americans With Disabilities Act* since they are mainly designed to diagnose abnormal behavioral patterns. The *ADA* states that an employer "shall not conduct a medical examination or make inquiries as to whether such applicant is an individual with a disability or as to the nature and severity of such disability."

In 1989, a class-action lawsuit was filed on behalf of security applicants at *Target's* 113 California stores. The plaintiff was an individual who applied for a security guard position with *Target* stores and was required to take the *California Psychological Inventory* (*CPA*) and the *Minnesota Multiphasic Personality Inventory* (*MMPI*). He contended that the test questions probed into his private thoughts and deepest feelings and were not job related. The court agreed that some of the test questions did indeed invade the applicants' privacy because they asked about religious beliefs and sexual preferences. Among the true/false questions were:

- I believe my sins are unpardonable.
- I am very attracted to members of my own sex.
- Evil spirits possess me sometimes.
- I have no difficulty starting or holding my bowel movement.
- My sex life is satisfactory.
- I have never been in trouble because of my sexual behavior.
- I feel sure there is only one true religion.
- I go to church almost every week.

Target needed to show some compelling reasons for the invasion of privacy and demonstrate that the test served a job-related purpose to justify that invasion of privacy. While the court acknowledged that *Target* had an interest in employing emotionally stable persons as security officers, *Target* did not show how information pertaining to an applicant's sexual preferences or religious beliefs would have any bearing on emotional stability. Therefore, the questions were deemed as not being job-related. *Target* settled the lawsuit for over $2 million without admitting wrongdoing or liability.

Most companies and their hiring managers would understand they could not legally ask those same questions directly in an applicant interview. That would represent an unlawful inquiry. As a general rule of thumb, there's very little legal difference in asking the question in an interview or soliciting the response from an assessment questionnaire.

A good reference on the use of assessments has been published by the *U.S. Department of Labor*. It's titled, *Testing and Assessment: An Employer's Guide to Good Practice*. The book gives a terrific overview of the many different types of assessments, legal implications, test quality, test selection, administration, scoring and interpretation.

My own view of assessments is fairly nuanced. They can help a hiring manager or team identify individual SUCCESS STYLES including motivations and preferences at work. I am careful not to use the word "test" even though it is a popular term to describe these tools. The simple reason is that "test" often suggests a right or wrong answer or category. These tools don't measure right or wrong on anything. They are only designed to suggest tendencies that might help a recruiter choose an applicant that is better suited to a role based on their innate style. The best profiles are rated at about an 80% validity rate. That means that on average, results are 20% inaccurate. At the end of the day these tools can be extremely useful to "tee up" or begin an ongoing conversation with an applicant on where they might fit best.

A psychometric indicator does a reasonable job suggesting "how" a candidate is likely to be the most successful at a given task or position. They might also be suggestive of "what" you will be good at. None of the indicators pretend to describe a candidate entirely. Each indicator provides only a single window to see who they are. Never let any person or any assessment define a candidate with a declarative statement.

• **Indicators can offer an idea of candidate strengths**
• **Indicators can help a candidate target specific career niches**

Work sample indicators can do a reasonable job of assessing for skill level. Cognitive ability indicators can be helpful measuring things like verbal reasoning or numeric reasoning.

"The most important skill any business person can develop is interviewing… It calls for a unique skill set, and the simple truth is most people are not good at it."

~Eric Schmidt

Chapter Seventeen
Audition - Strengths Based Interviewing

Companies like *Toyota, Apple, Google* and *Facebook* look for Passion, Talent, Personality, Character and Values as well as Skills and Knowledge. I recommend constructing a Strengths Matrix to identify what/who you need on the team.

Strengths Based Resume Sorting & Reading

In Joel Spolsky's *Smart and Gets Things Done,* he has a whole chapter on sorting resumes from his perspective, hiring people in the tech industry. Spolsky shares how he reads a resume looking for candidate passion. He looks for evidence that the applicant loves computers and programming. Some specific examples include:

1- Jobs with computers or experience programming going back to a very early age. Spolsky believes that great programmers are more likely to have spent a summer at computer camp, or building an online appointment scheduler for their uncle the dentist, rather than working at *Banana Republic* folding clothes.

2- Extra-Curricular Activities. People who love programming often work on their own programming projects (or contribute to an open source project) in their spare time.

3- Waxing rhapsodic in their cover letter about how they were moved to tears by *Structure and Interpretation of Computer Programs*. (a book by Harold Abelson with Gerald and Julie Sussman)

4- Sometimes certain programming languages or technologies on a resume indicate evidence of someone who loves programming enough to explore new technologies. Seeing *Ruby* on a resume (In 2012) is a good sign of the kind of programmer who loves to check out the latest thing. It shows they are trying to improve their skills and indicates a passion about programming. In other words, they're working with Ruby before employers are demanding it. Spolsky cautions, "You have to be careful here; in 1996, *Java* on a resume was a sign of the same passion, but today it almost adds no information."

Spolsky continues, "We look closely at the cover letter for evidence that the applicant really wants to work for us. We don't want to see a generic cover letter talking about me, me, me: we want to see a coherent argument as to why they've thought about this seriously and concluded that *Fog Creek* is the place they want to work… A custom cover letter is a sign that if we do make this candidate an offer, they're likely to accept it. That improves our yield. If I only have time to interview six people, all else being equal, I'd rather interview six people who really want to work for *Fog Creek*."

On the talent side, Spolsky says he looks for a particular kind of smart. "Signs of this include high GPAs, high standardized test scores, honor societies like *Phi Beta Kappa*, people who participate in *Top Coder* competitions, play competitive chess, or go to *ACM Programming* contests."

Obviously this is what you might look for when hiring people to write computer code. Please don't generalize… You would have missed the whole point of the strengths message that is central to this book. Take this information and adapt it for signs of passion and talent for the roles you are hiring.

The Strengths Based Phone Screen

If you have a lot of qualified candidates, a good phone screen can save you the time and trouble of interviewing the least qualified candidates. On the other hand, if you don't have a lot of qualified candidates to interview, a phone screen could pre-maturely remove a great candidate because they don't feel comfortable on the phone. I recommend choosing three questions off of the strengths oriented application that was discussed in an earlier section. Read the question and reflect back your understanding of their answer, then drill deeper, ask if there is anything else the candidate would like to explain or elaborate on.

First Question

My favorite opening interview question is one that I got from a fellow hiring manager. I don't think the brilliance of it can be understated. And it can be used as a first question in both the phone screen and the first interview.

"WHAT ATTRACTED YOU TO THE AD or POSITION?"

Take detailed notes on the answer! The answers you receive to this question will give you feedback that allows you to tweak your job posting. Beyond that, it is a wide-open question that begins the strengths discovery process. With some follow-up and drill-down, the question will solicit the images of the job the person has floating around in their head. Follow-up questions like: **"What's Important About That?"** or **"How Did That Part of The Job Description Connect With You?"** should give you some great insight on a candidate's Passion/Deeply Embedded Interest as well as their Talent/Aptitudes. Don't beat the question up, but don't be afraid to follow-up and mine it for all it's worth.

Interview Questions

Facebook is widely known to use a key strengths based question as a signature part of their interview process:

"On your very best day at work – the day you come home and think you have the very best job in the world – what did you do that day?"

According to *Facebook* executive Miranda Kalinowski, "When we ask the question, we're looking to see what the candidate is truly passionate about and whether that innate interest fits into what *Facebook* is looking for." The answer to that question will tell you so much whether you are selecting for overall employment or putting together the next project team.

You'll want to collect and develop a series of strengths based questions for each of the positions you interview for. Here is another question, this one formulated by Dan Sullivan:

"What is the single focus and activity that would keep you absolutely fascinated and motivated for the rest of your life?"

Another question, this one by Peter Bregman:

"What do you do in your time off?"

Bregman expands on this question with an exploration of Captain C.B. Sullenberger's use of non-working hours. As we all know, Sully made an emergency landing of his fifty-ton aircraft on the Hudson River in New York City on January 15, 2009. In doing this, he effectively saved the lives of 155 people on board.

Bregman asks a provocative question about this event. Was it miraculous or was it predictable? In other words, could Sullenberger's successful actions that day have been predicted in an interview? Bregman suggests it was predictable, had the interviewer asked, "What do you do in your time off?"

Bregman theorizes, "The first clue that he would become Captain Sullenberger the hero is that, in his teens, when most of his friends were getting their driver's licenses, he got his pilot's license. What did he do for fun? He flew glider planes, which is basically what he did when he landed in the Hudson River with no engines. Extracurricular activities? He was an accident investigator for the *Airline Pilots Association* and worked with federal aviation officials to improve training methods for evacuating aircraft in emergencies. As a boy, he built model aircraft carriers with tiny planes on them, careful to paint every last piece."

Bregman concludes, "Obsessions are one of the greatest telltale signs of success. Understand obsessions and you will understand natural motivation."

These last words suggest another great interview question. Ask the candidate, "**What are you obsessed with?"**

Strengths Based Interview Questions (By Category)

The following are some great questions that will help you discover a candidate's strengths in the areas we have discussed. Many were also included on the Strengths Oriented Application mentioned earlier. I actually recommend taking their written application and using it as an interview guide. This ensures there are no trick questions. As the hiring manager you are playing all your cards face up. This gives the candidate full opportunity to prepare for the first interview and builds trust.

The *Facebook* Interview Question (This has been explained thoroughly.) "On your very best day at work, the day you come home and think you have the very best job in the world, what did you do that day?"

The Miracle Question? This is a hiring version coming from *Solution Oriented Behavioral Therapy* - Imagine waking up tomorrow morning, and everything about your job is changing. Your work is shifting to something amazing. What exactly are you seeing, hearing and feeling? Most importantly, what are you doing? How are you doing it? Where are you doing it? Who are you collaborating with? How do you recognize that this is in fact your dream job?

Interviewing for Contribution – Key Results

What is your most important accomplishment/contribution?

What strengths show up when you walk in the room?

What are your contributions?

Where do you add value?

Where do positive results show up as a result of your activities?

What is the role or roles where you have been indispensible?

What tasks are you invited to perform? When do people ask you back?

What are your "Encore Activities" where people want a repeat performance?

Interviewing for Passion

I recommend reviewing the "Image Gathering" exercise in the chapter titled, *Staffing for Passion* as well as the section, *"Get Them Going"*.

What are your dreams?

What's your "I'd rather be" bumper sticker?

Which sections of the bookstore/magazine section pull you?

Where do you spend money after the bills are paid?

What are your regular online stops?

What do you do with your free time?

What do you do after work and on weekends?

What gets you going?

What activities give you energy?

What are your "Lights On" subjects?

Which topics of discussion light you up?

What are your daydreams?

What are you always thinking about?

What's stewing in your mental crock pot?

What's on your calendar? What do you schedule?

What are your favorite movies or TV shows?

Interviewing for Talent

Identify your *"Factory Settings"*. What did you love doing at ages 5, 6, 7, 8, 9, 10, 11, 12, 13, 14? What were you good at?

What activities and tasks do you have an instinctive feel for? What's your version of a "green thumb"?

Someone has said we all have about 20,000 moments a day. What are your "Made-For-This-Moments"? What are the times or activities where you felt like you were made to do that?

What activities do you find *impossible* not to get involved with? What can't you not do?

What are you insanely great at?

Where or when are you the most creative?

What are the situations where you come up with ideas?

When do you easily go off script and improvise?

What do you see or notice that other people don't?

In what areas or activities do you grow the fastest?

What are the subjects you learned quickly and easily?

What are the skills you picked up without much effort?

What is your genius?

How are you smart?

Which of your talents aren't getting used?

List the following intelligences in order as you think they show up in your personal hierarchy.

Word Smart? Picture Smart? Body Smart? Logic/Math Smart? People Smart? Self Smart? Nature Smart? Existential Smart? Music Smart?

What's inside of you trying to get out? What activities must you do?

Are you better at Execution, Influence, Relationship Building or Strategic Thinking? List them in order.

Interviewing for Personality Traits

How would you describe yourself?

What symbol or symbols would you use to describe yourself? !?@#$&<>/=+-

Do you ponder or socialize? Are you intra-active or interactive?

Do you prefer to use your intuition or your five senses?

Do you like plans and structure or making it up as you go?

Do you prefer to go solo or with a partner?

What are your quirks?

Interview for Values & Cultural Fit

An ideal world/work/workplace would have more…?

Tangibly, what would that look like?

What's important to you in a job?

How would you describe your philosophy?

What are the wrongs in the world that must be set right? What makes you angry?

What traditional belief would you most like to challenge?

What is difficult for you to tolerate?

What day-to-day irritations do you experience?

Interviewing for Knowledge

What kind of information just seems to jump in your head?

What subjects are you an expert in?

Who are your current or past teachers, trainers or coaches?

If you had to teach a subject, what would it be?

Where is your vocabulary or terminology the strongest?

What is your biggest area of ignorance?

What subjects are you most curious about?

Interviewing for Skills

If your life depended on naming a skill at which you're in the top 1% of the world, what would it be?

What skill would you enjoy increasing 25% in the next year?

Where are you still trying to grow and get better?

Where do you need to grow?

If there was one thing you'd start doing differently tomorrow to unleash more of your potential, what would it be?

What have you learned how to do? If you had to train or coach someone, what would it be?

What is your magic tool? …Something like a wand that allows you to work magic?

For Harold, in the children's book by Crockett Johnson, it was his Purple Crayon.

For Picasso, it was a paint brush.

For Jimi Hendrix, it was his guitar that he reportedly slept with.

For Dr. Ben Carson, it was a scalpel.

For Steph Curry, it's a basketball behind the 3-Point line.

Interviewing for Character

Where are you the best at keeping your commitments?

When do you not keep your commitments?

What internal direction or calling have you ignored?

What do you do without thinking?

Interviewing for Other Strengths

What's your chronotype?

Imagine you extended your life 10 years or could do a set of activities for eternity. What is your vision of paradise on earth? What about that vision really captivates you?

Who are your role models or heroes? Who would you like to be more like?

Are these role models symbolic or do you actually want to do what they do each day?

What's the best thing about you that very few people know?

What is your superpower?

What is your kryptonite/biggest weakness?

Auditions & Tryouts

In an article for *Wired* magazine, *Google's* Lazlo Block offers a summary of the 1998 research conducted by Frank Schmidt and John Hunter. It was a meta-analysis of 85 years of research on how well different hiring methods predict performance. Block shares that they looked at 19 different assessment techniques and found that typical, unstructured job interviews were pretty bad at predicting how someone would perform once hired.

• Unstructured interviews explain 14 percent of performance.

• Reference checks explain 7 percent of performance.

• Work experience explains 3 percent.

The best predictor of how someone will perform in a job is a work sample test (29 percent). This entails giving candidates a sample piece of work, similar to that which they would do in the job, and assessing their performance at it. Even this can't predict performance perfectly, since actual performance also depends on other skills, such as how well you collaborate with others, adapt to uncertainty, and learn.

Is it possible that *Little League* Baseball has a more effective selection system than corporate America? I still remember my *Little League* tryout. I was 11 years old. During the tryout on two successive Saturdays, the coaches from all of the teams in the league were there. They hit us ground balls and fly balls. They watched us bat. As I graduated to the *Babe Ruth* League with older kids, the system got a little more sophisticated but had about the same components. And everyone didn't make the team. The middle school team and then the high school teams got a bit more sophisticated still. The tryouts lasted for a few weeks and included situations and scrimmage games.

Theater and music productions worked similarly. You had to tryout. You had to actually play the instrument, sing the song or read for the part. Can you imagine using an interview to select Joanne or Johnny for any of these roles? Not a chance. Does the *Little League* coach and the Theater Arts teacher know something that the average hiring manager or human resource director has forgotten?

This syncs up perfectly with Schmidt and Hunter's 1998 research paper doesn't it? Isn't an audition or tryout the same thing as a work sample?

My advice is to structure your interview using the categories and questions in the previous pages. Then develop a great work sample that is job specific.

Moneyball

Before we leave baseball too quickly, let's look at another example. Beyond the issue of selection methods, there is the issue of identifying the elements that drive success. Historically, baseball scouts looked for players based on five factors – Running, Throwing, Catching, Batting Average and Home Runs. These five factors were the foundation for finding and signing great baseball talent. Then, a baseball general manager named Billy Beane dug a little deeper into the data. What he discovered has changed baseball recruiting forever. Beane found that one additional factor, On-Base-Percentage, was actually more predictive of team contribution and winning baseball games than Batting Average and

Home Runs. By changing his team's scouting, assessment and draft strategy to more closely match what actually drove winning baseball games, the team was immediately able to win more league division championships. The detailed story of *Moneyball* is outlined in the book by Michael Lewis. The book was turned into a feature film by same name. It stars Brad Pitt as Billy Beane.

Create Your Nine Panel Strengths Based Hiring Summary

Strengths Hiring Summary

Contribution – Key Results - Outcomes		
Passion	Talent	Personality
Values	Learning Style	Knowledge
Skills	Character	Other

Helping a Candidate Describe Themselves

Business author Tom Peters said, "You had better have a clear mark of distinction brilliantly communicated." Management Consultant Peter Drucker said, "Most Americans do not know what their strengths are. When you ask them, they look at you with a blank stare…"

Ultimately you want to help a candidate succeed at accurately describing themselves. A Strengths Oriented Interview should not have even one "Gotcha Moment". You may overlook the best candidate because they don't know how to respond to your clever little question. You may overlook the best candidate for a position just because they haven't learned how to describe, demonstrate and display their strengths. The purpose of your interview is NOT to figure out how well the person interviews unless the position is related to oral communications or sales.

Have Them Share a S.T.A.R. Story Paragraph

S.T.A.R. stands for **S**trength, **T**arget, **A**ction, **R**esult. Have the candidate share a short Success Story about themselves from work, school, sports, a hobby or volunteer activity. Instruct the applicant to write a sentence for each of the four points:

Strength you used

Target you defined

Action you took

Result you achieved

Multiple Interviews & Multiple Locations

Tony Robbins says his organization interviews multiple times in different locations, including the candidate's home. "We want to see how you live. I want to see what it's like to walk inside your house. I want to get in your car, because that tells me a lot."

Increasingly, good companies are interviewing multiple times, up to four even for introductory level jobs. Some companies always include a restaurant interview. Some use a golf or sports outing or event.

Interview Exercise Examples

The following are interview exercises that organizations use. They can make the interview process more fun and memorable and offer other kinds of information you wouldn't receive in more standard formats.

Interview Request: You have 15 minutes to design a creative resume. You can use no words. (Flip chart size paper was supplied with colored markers.)

4-Hour Work Sample Interview: Some companies are paying candidates to come in and work an actual shift as part of the interview or selection process.

4-Hour, 9-Person, Panel Interview: Some companies are conducting very lengthy interviews with multiple staff present and asking questions. (I spoke with a candidate who answered questions from nine people for four hours. This was an introductory position.)

Interview - 1 Leader, 12 Observers, 16 Interviewees Divided Into Teams of 4:

Toy animals were on each table for team mascots. Candidates were asked to build a tower with index cards and tooth picks. Colored pens and index cards for name decorations were provided. Each candidate was given 20 seconds to introduce themselves and why they chose that decoration. A bell signaled the end of the 20 seconds. The interview leader asked questions that included:

- What are the most populous countries?
- What are the top 10 animals that cause human death?
- What are the top 10 grossing movies?
- Math questions involving money.
- Logic questions.
- Math word problems.
- Alphabetize ten names.
- Write two complete sentences describing the week's weather.

Prizes - Bags of candy, bouncing balls and *Dollar Store* items were awarded. Wine and cheese was served at the end. The interview was 1.5 hours start to finish including a facility tour.

"The most important decisions businesspeople make are not 'what' decisions but 'who' decisions."

~Jim Collins

Chapter Eighteen
Appointments: Making The Selection

Kip Tindell, in his book *Uncontainable*, talks about the hiring philosophy at *The Container Store*, "Hiring people who will be naturally drawn to the tasks within a role is known as Strengths-Based Recruitment. 1=3. 1 Great Person = 3 Good People. 1 Equals 3 is our hiring philosophy. We have to be selective when interviewing potential employees because of the brand promise we've made to our customers to provide exceptional customer service. We only hire 3% of all who apply. If you indeed believe that with one great employee, you get three times the productivity of a good employee, you can afford to extensively train them and communicate to them, empower them and pay them 50 to 100% more than other retailers might pay them. Our 1=3 employees have tremendous tenure with the company. They feel like owners of the company and strive to do what's right for each other and our customers every single day. It's a win-win. Employees win because they're getting paid twice as much... and what a delight for the entire team to work alongside other great people! The company wins because it gets three times the productivity at two times the payroll cost. But most importantly, customers win with extraordinary service!"

The Hiring Packet

Google has developed a Hiring Packet, a single standardized comprehensive document that includes all the known information about a candidate that has progressed through the hiring process. They use it across job functions and across continents, no matter where they are hiring. Listed below are some of the components that may be found in the Hiring Packet document depending on the position:

One-Page Candidate Summary

Key Facts

Supporting Material – All opinions must include "documented proof"

Interview Reports – Includes Best & Worst Answers

Resume – Includes Typos and Formatting Errors

Compensation History

Reference Information

College Transcripts

Copy of Patents

Copy of Awards

Writing Samples

Coding Samples

Grade Point Average – Specifying American 4.0 System or Other

Class Ranking

The *Google* Hiring Packet was designed by engineers and always is the final decision maker. Department managers have veto power, but not hiring power which is delegated to a hiring team. None of the team members have met the candidate. Best Packet Wins!

Does this level of detail make sense for the average start-up, micro-business or small business? Maybe not, but it might offer some good steps that could be implemented with the first hire.

Appearances

When I say, "appearances", I mean more than just looks. I mean the whole individual impact. It's how the candidate seems to "land" or come across. Stereotypes and stereotypical expectations really come into play here.

Teri and Michelle were hired as marketing reps for two Northern California sales territories. For some reason there was a lot of debate about these two candidates, which one would last? Which one would excel? By appearance, Teri had all of the earmarks of a top outside salesperson. She was the most aggressive, outgoing and by far the favorite based on stereotypical factors. Michelle was more reserved. But she also had extensive affinity and background with the type of accounts we were selling into. She was a much better cultural fit with the accounts. Teri lasted about a year, while Michelle went on to be a company leader. Be careful with stereotypical beliefs about who succeeds and fails within a given role. The questions should be asked, "Selling What?" "Selling Where?" "Selling to Who?"

Again, be wary of making judgments based on "looks" or attractiveness. Even in positions where attractiveness would seem to matter, I've seen more unattractive candidates excel. This is a benefit of the *Google* Hiring Packet. The people making the final decisions haven't even seen the person.

The Cost of A Bad Hire or Position Left Open

When I was hired as a West Coast sales manager, I was told that hiring was the most important thing I did. I took that very seriously. I was also told that every time a position opened up, it cost the company 30 or 40K. I have no idea where that number came from but I believe it could have been conservative, maybe quite conservative. Even a couple of lost accounts could have meant losing that much in gross revenue. And the lost follow-up and customer service probably meant lost business two and three years down the road. There was also a discontinuity of customer relationships.

Our organization always thought in terms of the cost of a position left open. But I also thought in terms of the cost of bad hire. A bad hire could mean many things and I cleaned up my fair share of messes. A bad hire in our context could cost hundreds of thousands of dollars in the next sales cycle two or three years later. The organization could lose a customer for a decade or even for life. During my years as a sales representative, there were accounts a previous representative had underserved that took me my whole tenure to win back. There were others I never did. Good hiring is good business!

Selling The Company and The Position

For eight years I was a hiring manager for a large national company on the West Coast. I regularly hired employees from San Diego to Seattle and many places in between. During my first set of interviews, a candidate came in who interviewed perfectly. I badly wanted to hire the applicant. It never occurred to me they wouldn't take the position. I wasn't prepared to sell my industry, my company or the position to this highly qualified candidate. Could I have persuaded her to join our company? We'll never know. What I do know is that too many hiring managers insist on taking the position that they are the ones who are doing the candidate a big favor. And this attitude costs them the most qualified candidates. The best candidates have options.

You may need to sell a candidate on the value of your whole industry…The "Dead End Job Deception" is pervasive in today's American culture and it comes in at least four versions. Americans believe that certain jobs have no future.

I believe there are people wandering around disconnected from their unique destiny because they have bought into this deception. Many are hoping to do something important with their life, like play basketball or become a rocket scientist, all the while their true genius is in fast food operations, retail or somehow working with their hands. They could have been working at the C-Suite level at *In-n-Out Burger* if they had just been willing to start flipping burgers. They could have been working at the C-Suite level at *Nordstrom* had they just been willing to fold and stock clothes. They could have ran their own *Harley-Davidson* dealership had they just been willing to get their hands greasy on a motorcycle chain. Or they could have set up a very successful farming operation had they believed it was worth starting in the fields.

I recommend putting together a few stories about people who have succeeded wildly in your industry. Be completely honest but be prepared to romance the opportunity when you honestly believe you have a mutually beneficial job fit.

Assemble a nice package of information about the company. Interview in an attractive environment.

"Experience is <u>not</u> the best teacher; evaluated experience is the best teacher."

~John Maxwell

Chapter Nineteen
Autopsy Your Process

Some of the most successful television shows and novel characters have centered on the autopsy. When I was growing up, Jack Klugman played *Quincy*. Patricia Cornwall's novels featured Dr. Kay Scarpetta and more recently we've had the *CSI* shows. Susy and I both loved the quirky Max Bergman in the new iteration of Hawaii Five-O. The basic idea is to identify cause of death. In criminal cases, clues are discovered. In regular medicine, the focus might be on learning, future prevention and an advancement in medicine that will save lives.

Much of my work has been deconstructing both successes and failures. When I was a sales manager I put together a "Lost Sale Autopsy" form that encouraged my team to reflect on their wins and losses looking for clues that might accelerate success. The tool walked them through the steps of our sales cycle presentation. As a group, salespeople aren't always the most reflective bunch and I seriously doubt it got a lot of use. But if you're serious about success in any arena, career, weight loss or even relationships; an autopsy can get you back on track.

Debrief every hiring sequence. Debrief every interview!!!

What went well?

What went okay?

What went poorly?

What do you wish you would have said?

As a hiring manager and potential employer, you can recover from some mistakes. If you're fortunate enough to get a second interview, that would be one kind of recovery opportunity. A strong post interview thank you follow-up is another opportunity. Every single time an employee leaves your organization do an exit interview. Learn – Learn – Learn!!! Improve – Improve – Improve.

It is sometimes erroneously assumed that top performers don't make many mistakes and therefore rarely look back. Top winners never dwell on mistakes. They don't beat themselves up. But they do review. At nearly every level, including high school, college and professional football, the day after the game is set aside for watching film of the previous day's performance.

Basketball start Kobe Bryant talks about his relationship with assistant Coach Tex Winter who he referred to as Yoda. Bryant shares, "We'd sit together and we'd watch film of every game. The first time we sat down and watched film I was kinda like we're going to watch my touches. No. We'd watch the game from start to finish, rewinding it, looking at plays, looking at tactics… start to finish, every game... Every game. I liked it. I started picking things. I started playing the game and now when things are going at a fast pace I was able to slow the game down and see exactly what I was seeing on the screen. The game seemed much slower to me. And now I can also manipulate the game. I can think three, four, five moves ahead. I could put people in their right positions and organize things."

Dr. John Maxwell believes that there are several places the wheels come off in the staffing process. Here are a few examples.

1- Failure to know the requirements needed to make a job successful. Maxwell is not talking about the job description, and he's not talking about how the employee performs a job. He's talking about the activities and the corresponding traits an associate needs to be successful. Maxwell suggests making a list of those qualities. It could be two or three things, it could be 10. Whatever those things are, go out and find people who have the gifts and talents to match the position. Get the right people in the right place.

2- Failure to know the skills and the giftedness of the person. Maxwell suggests that sometimes we know what gifts and skills are required for success in a particular job, but we do a poor job evaluating the giftedness of the candidates we assess for the position. For example, maybe it's clear that a particular job needs someone who is detail-oriented, but the hiring process doesn't effectively assess candidates for that quality.

3- **Failure to move people when either the job or the person is changing.** We are in a rapidly changing world. What it takes to perform a position effectively in one decade may not be the same thing it takes to perform in the next. In some cases, the change can even take place in two or three years. I was a sales manager when our company made the transition from 3x5 cards to the *Salesforce.com* customer relationship manager (CRM). We had representatives that never were able to make the transition. It required a slightly different set of aptitudes and complimentary skills.

4- Failure to be patient. Maxwell believes that some employees are placed correctly but they need some extra time to grow and develop. This may also require extra training or different training. They have the talent, they have the skills, they have the passion; but they need time and someone to help them.

5- Failure to prepare. Preparation makes everything better! Many times we haven't done enough front-end homework as hiring managers. We haven't taken time to really understand the requirements of the position or investigated ways to assess who has those qualities. Maxwell talks about the downward spiral, "Morale suffers, people lose their willingness to play as a team and confidence erodes." But there is the upward spiral as well, Maxwell adds, "Organizations do best when the people within them are carefully put in the right places. People are encouraged and fulfilled, growth is ensured, teamwork is increased and victories are secured."

Helping Your People Shift Roles

Sometimes people have to change jobs to realize their potential. Maybe you've hired them to work for the best company in the world. But maybe they're in the wrong role. You hired them for sales but they really belong in marketing. You hired them for management but they really belong in training.

Have you heard of Babe Ruth? Unless you're a baseball fan maybe not. If you have heard of him, you may know he's considered by some to be the best baseball hitter of all time. But unless you are among the most dedicated of baseball fans, you may not know that he started his professional career as a pitcher. He was a very good pitcher too. But at one point in his professional career, he made the decision to stop pitching so he could focus on a role where he was even better. **He was even heavily criticized for the decision**. Looking back, it was a pretty good choice. His decision to set aside the role of pitcher, where he was merely good, in favor of a role where he could become the world's greatest hitter, was life changing for him and his teammates.

Do you have someone on your team who would benefit from the "Babe Ruth" strategy? Do you need to figure out how to help them let go of tasks and activities where they don't have the potential to become the best? Maybe they need to be in another position all together. Or maybe they need to expand or reduce a current role.

Strengths Strategist Marcus Buckingham estimates that as many as 80% of U.S. workers are in a role or position that needs adjustment if they are to maximize their performance and contribution in the workplace. About 1/3 of that 80% are **playing the wrong position all together.** A second 1/3 would perform much better if they were **working in a pared down or more focused version of their current role.** And a final 1/3 would actually contribute more if they worked in a **more expanded version of their current role.**

What about your team?

Often the difference between being good and being great is making adjustments that allow team members to spend more of their time delivering their greatest strengths.

Have you ever conducted an annual performance review where the focus quickly shifted to a discussion about how to fix your associate's weaknesses? It's an all-too-common scenario. And it's probably a waste of time. It's a much better idea to build on their strengths.

Do you want your team to go from good to great? Focus on their natural talents and passions. Why? Because you will develop faster and better, doing what they do best and enjoy most. These are their strengths and they are theirs for life.

You can build on them, and they won't let the team down. Think about it: What would their life be like if they got paid to do what they do best and truly enjoy? Awesome thought isn't it?

"At its root, Scrum is based on a simple idea: whenever you start a project, why not regularly check in, see if what you're doing is heading in the right direction. And question whether there are any ways to improve how you're doing what you're doing, any ways of doing it better and faster, and what might be keeping you from doing that."

~Jeff Sutherland

Chapter Twenty
Agile Hiring

Agile platforms are project management frameworks originating at *Toyota*, and now being implemented by thousands of individuals, teams and organizations in all types of industries all over the world. In 1986, it took *General Motors* 40 hours to manufacture a car with an average of 13 defects per car. In the same year, *Toyota* could manufacture an equal car in 18 hours with 4.5 defects. What allowed *Toyota* to outperform *General Motors* at this level? There was only one significant difference. *Toyota* had been using an *Agile project management* framework known as *Lean*. In recent years, *General Motors* has used *Lean* to completely close that gap.

Building contractors now use *Agile* as do farmers, classroom teachers and wedding planners. *National Public Radio Teams* began using *Agile* strategies during the chaotic events of the Arab Spring. It spread throughout *NPR* and then to teams at the *Washington Post*, *New York Times* and *Chicago Tribune*. The *Grameen Foundation* is using *Agile* methodologies to eliminate poverty in Uganda.

Agile has diversified into multiple frameworks including *Extreme Programing*, *Kanban*, and *Scrum*. You can transform your hiring management using the same project management framework that the world's top companies are using to build products and services.

There are several benefits of the *Agile* framework. It's extremely flexible as the name implies and it's simple to start using. But when the need is there, it can expand into a very sophisticated set of tools. It can be used individually or with teams. If you are already using one of the *Agile* platforms in a work context, this will build on something you already understand. If you're not familiar with *Agile*, this provides a brief introduction that may benefit you later.

For a primer on *Agile Scrum*, I recommend Jeff Sutherland's book, *Scrum – The Art of Doing Twice the Work in Half the Time*. This is not your typical time management book. For a deeper dive, download the *SBOK Guide* or *Scrum Body of Knowledge*. It's free online. For an introduction to *Lean*, I recommend, *A Factory of One* by Daniel Markovitz.

On the following pages, I'm going to offer a very basic overview of *Agile*. I'm going to share six components. They are **Kanban Board, Sprint, Sprint Planning, Daily Scrum, Sprint Review and Sprint Retrospective**. If you want to start simply, for hiring management, just focus on the Kanban Board. This will offer a super simple fast start. (I am intentionally capitalizing all the *Agile* specific language that may be new to you.)

Kanban Board

"Write the vision and make it plain on tablets, that he may run who reads it."
~Habakkuk 2:2

Great time managers use scoreboards and dashboards to keep everyone aware of progress. Carl Pearson was the father of modern business statistics and is known for Pearson's Law: "When performance is measured, performance improves" and the corollary: "When performance is measured and reported, it improves exponentially." This is true even at the international economic level. The countries that measure and quantify have the strongest thriving economies.

In *Agile*, the project to-do list (called a Back-Log List) goes on a "Do" - "Doing" - "Done" board that is often referred to by the Japanese name Kanban (meaning "Card You Can See"). In the Scrum framework, it goes by ScrumBoard.

I like the "Do" – "Doing" – "Done" format because it perfectly matches the **Y.E.S.** time frames I use in passion assessment. Is there a **Yearning** before you begin the items on the "Do" list? Is there **Engagement** with a growing sense of energy and timelessness while you're "Doing" the items? Is there a sense of **Satisfaction** after you've "Done" the items on the list? The Kanban Board can provide a terrific strengths check-in.

You can easily build your own Kanban on a sheet of paper, poster board, grease board or using an online tool. If you go with the online option, I recommend *Trello.com* which is what I use. It's easy to learn and can be reconfigured and shared easily.

HIRE (DO)	HIRING (DOING)	HIRED (DONE)

Hiring Sprints

A Sprint is a time-boxed process of one month or less, where an individual or team implements a goal-oriented Backlog of Tasks. A common Sprint length is 21 days but it can be up to 30 days or as little as one week. If you're just introducing the concept, you can shorten your Sprint length to a single day or even an hour or less for a walk-through or training purposes. You can also combine it with the *Pomodoro* concept to work with 25 minute increments.

The idea of a Sprint is to completely finish an increment of a project. A Hiring Sprint could be completing a phase of hiring, completing a set of job descriptions or writing and posting advertisements for 21 days. The Sprint is all about having specific demonstrated results at the end. Some *Lean* practitioners use the term MVP for Minimum Viable Product to describe the end result. Minimum in this case does not refer to cutting corners or short cuts. It refers to delivering each project increment with a fully functional useable product or service. By keeping the Sprint length short, course corrections and hiring phase responsive adjustments can be made.

Sprint Planning

Each Sprint begins with a planning session. In the world of software design, a planning session for a 21 day Sprint might take 8 hours. You may spend much less time if you're using the *Agile* method for hiring management. I recommend the 1-week Sprint time frame in the beginning. When planning a Sprint segment, consider the **S.P.R.I.N.T.S.** acrostic below that is loosely built on the *Agile* pattern. Most of these ideas are pulled from the *Agile Scrum* family but some are pulled from *Lean.*

Story Map

Agile planning begins with a focus on how the product/service will add value to a specific end user. If you are an HR person, your end user may be a hiring manager or product team. *Agile* planning starts with a 3-step **User Story** that is often placed on a simple 3x5 index card.
I am… Who is the client, customer or end user or what is their role? (Example: Hiring Manager, Team Leader, CEO)
I want… What does the end user want the product/service to achieve for them? (Example: Hire Coder, Salesperson, Executive Secretary)
So that… What will be the benefit of that? (Example: Complete Software Project, Increase Sales, Increase Support)

A Story Map includes a description of what will be delivered to the client or customer. *Agile* planning is very big on providing a very clear definition of "Done". The "Done" criteria should include quality standards. (Example: Software Coder will include strong aptitudes – Spatial Visualization and Skills - Ruby.)

Deliverables are what will be delivered and demonstrated at the end of each Sprint. *Agile* often creates a Project Vision Statement that explains the business need that will be met or what problem will be solved. (Example: We are creating a new software to enhance document preparation. Hiring the additional coder will accelerate the project and allow us to deliver on time.)

Agile planning is very big on providing a very clear definition of "Done". The "Done" criteria should include quality standards. (Example: Software coder will be hired by Date and on-boarded by Date) Story Maps are often used to give a visual outline of the hiring project sequence. This is similar to Storyboarding used by *Disney*. Value Stream Mapping may be used to identify non-value adding elements of a process.

Problems

A SWOT Analysis or a Force Field Analysis may be incorporated to identify potential obstacles and trouble. Threats are risks that could affect a project in a negative manner.

The Bruce Tuckman Norming-Forming-Storming-Performing group process model is often used to identify potential team conflicts.

In the *Lean* framework, Plan-Do-Check-Act may be implemented with problem solving. Other tools include the A-3 thinking and a tool called the 5 Whys. *Lean* adherents also follow the radical *Toyota* practice of allowing any worker on the assembly line to stop production and work on solving a problem.

Roles and Responsibilities

Agile planning then moves to identify the team members. In *Agile* Scrum the team has very specific names with very spelled out roles. I generally don't focus on the names like Scrum Master and Product Owner or Project Owner.

A Skills Requirement Matrix or framework can be used to identify skill gaps and training requirements for team members.

Agile is not inherently a strengths based project management system although many of the successful software companies like *Cisco* and *Facebook* are very strengths oriented. A basic tenet of Scrum is that all team members are cross-functional, that is, everyone has the skills necessary to complete any part of the Sprint. From a strengths perspective, this may not be optimal.

Agile projects can be completed without considering team member strengths and weaknesses. But virtually every top company, including *Toyota,* where the *Agile* concept was developed, is very strengths savvy. The tendency for mediocre companies is to focus solely on perceived skills as outlined on a resume and perceived knowledge as a function of a college degree. Great companies don't do that. Companies like *Toyota*, *Apple*, *Google* and *Facebook* look for Passion, Talent, Personality, Character and Values as well as Skills and Knowledge. I recommend constructing a Strengths Matrix to identify what/who you need on the team. *Facebook* is widely known to use a key strengths based question as a signature part of their interview process:

"On your very best day at work – the day you come home and think you have the very best job in the world – what did you do that day?"

The answer to that question will tell you so much whether you are hiring new employees or putting together the next project team.

Increments/Implementation/Iterations

Agile planning uses the term Iteration to describe the incremental segments within each Sprint. A Backlog or to-do list is built to describe the sequential tasks and activities that will go into the Sprint. These tasks go on a Burn Down Chart or Kanban Board that I will describe shortly. With the online option, I recommend *Trello.com* which is what I use. It's easy to learn and can be reconfigured and shared easily.

Niche Work Space

I include an emphasis on the space where the work will be done. *Agile Scrum* often refers to the work space as the **War Room**. It is optimally designed in a way that all team members can move freely, communicate and get their work done. Recently, there has been some criticism leveled at software development companies suggesting that the often used "open work" spaces do not provide an optimized environment for what Cal Newport and others call "deep work". This should be a consideration and a quiet, less interactive work space may be included in some cases.

The *Lean* family uses the Japanese term **Gemba** when talking about the space where value is created. Gemba could be the factory floor, a construction site, a farm, the desk where you write, the classroom where you teach, or the territory where you sell. *Apple's* retail store could be thought of as their Gemba. In case of Hiring, Gemba could be an interview room or an HR Office.

Time Estimate

Agile generally uses a team approach to estimating time and effort requirements on each Sprint. Estimating is not a top-down activity in *Agile*. The entire Sprint team is usually involved. Special *Agile* Poker Cards are often used as a method of identifying the amount of time that will be required for each task.

Sprint list Items may be identified by difficulty. Fibonacci sequence numbers are often used for this: 0,1,1, 2, 3, 5, 8, 13, 21 and so on.

Wideband Delphi Technique is used to describe an anonymous estimation process. Team members anonymously provide estimates for each product/service feature which in this case is a new hire. They then discuss factors influencing their time calculations and move on to a second round of anonymous estimates. The process is repeated until team members either develop consensus or get close to agreement.

Sprint Velocity is a term used to identify the rate at which the team can complete the work of a Sprint.

Productive Sustainable Pace suggests the rate a team can comfortably maintain.

S Framework

Agile Lean uses a methodology called *5S*. They have corresponding Japanese terms but the English terms are *Sort, Set Up, Sweep, Standardize* and *Sustain*.

Sort means throwing out useless or obsolete items and organizing the remaining items by frequency of use.

Set Up is arranging the tools and materials to promote a smooth workflow. In construction, I referred to this as staging the job.

Sweep is the maintenance phase and includes keeping the workspace clean. I would refer to it as *Struggle* because it's my weakness.

Standardize means developing a systematic ongoing work process. Standardizing in the *5S* sense is not static but open-ended, including ongoing improvements.

Sustain means having an ongoing system for maintaining and upgrading the first four elements.

Daily Scrum (Stand Up Meeting)

Agile teams have daily 15 minute standup meetings, often in front of the Kanban Board. *Trello* versions can be used for teams working remotely from different locations. The team reviews what was completed yesterday and previews what will be completed today. In some contexts, a set of four questions are used:

1. What has my team done since the last meeting?
2. What will my team do until the next meeting?
3. What are other teams counting on that remains undone?
4. What is the team doing that might affect other teams?

Some Scrum teams use a shorter three question model:

1. What did I complete yesterday?
2. What will I complete today?
3. What obstacles am I currently facing?

Sprint Review

The Sprint Review meeting, is typically structured to last 1 - 4 hours and is scalable up or down depending on the length of the Sprint. The purpose is to demonstrate or present the deliverables, usually to the Product Owner.

Sprint Retrospective

The Sprint Retrospective is typically structured to last 1 - 4 hours and is also scalable up or down depending on the length of the Sprint. The purpose is to review the process of that particular Sprint, identify what was learned, and suggest improvements for future Sprints.

Some *Agile* Sprints include a Retrospective Kanban with four categories: "Went Well", "Needs to Change", "Question & Discussion", "Action Items".

Speed Boat is a technique often used to identify the improvements. Team members play the role of a crew on a Speed Boat. The boat's goal is to reach an island which symbolizes the Project's Vision Statement. Sticky notes or index cards are used to identify the project's engines (accelerators) and anchors (drag). Engines are the things that helped the Sprint team reach the island and anchors are the things that slowed them down. This exercise is usually Time-Boxed to a few minutes in length.

More Exponential Results

It is so easy to get lulled into believing that individuals can be replaced like parts in a machine. With people, there are wide variations in strengths and performance.

Jeff Sutherland, co-founder of the *Scrum Project Management System* offers the following true story in his book titled *Scrum – The Art of Doing Twice the Work in Half the Time.*

Professor Stanley Eisenstat has been the instructor in the notoriously difficult, *Computer Science 323* course at *Yale University*.

Former student turned tech entrepreneur, Joel Spolsky wanted to know if there was any correlation between time spent on class projects and the grade received. Spolsky discovered there was no correlation, but the results were more interesting than that.

He found the fastest "A" students outpaced the slower "A" students by an incredible 10:1 margin. In other words, they were 10x faster on class projects and got just as good of a grade.

Rapid learning and work pace are strong indicators of innate talent. In a rapidly changing world, you will want to focus on careers where you can learn new material in the shortest time and where you can complete tasks quickly and efficiently.

Research shows an even greater gap. Sutherland references a team study that surveyed 3,800 different projects in a wide variety of fields. At the team level, variance range for exactly the same work project was one week to two thousand weeks.

Like individuals and teams, project management systems are not all equally effective. In 2010, *Federal Bureau of Investigation* agents were still filing most of their reports on paper. This issue was a substantial factor in the circumstances leading up to the attack on the *World Trade Center* nine years earlier. The first attempt to fix this was scrapped after three years and 70 million dollars of taxpayer money. The second attempt was projected to cost over 400 million dollars. *Agile* project management was finally used by a third team that fully delivered the project in 20 months at a fraction of the budget.

The *Healthcare.gov* rollout began with a similar disaster. The team who fixed it used *Agile Scrum*. Great people using an inferior project management system will produce less than spectacular results.

Amazon founder Jeff Bezos was asked what he believed were the greatest changes he saw coming in the next few years. Bezos responded, "That's a good question but a great question is what won't change in the next few years?" Bezos continued, "What won't change is the desire to get products and services faster and at a lower cost."

Bezos is correct. Both of those desires are timeless. Your ability as an individual and team member to deliver top talent faster and at a lower cost will always be in high demand. And they are a function of great hiring management.

"We're going to see more and more employment law action by the state and local governments on actions that have typically been the domain of the federal government."

~Labor and Employment Advanced Practices Symposium

Chapter Twenty One
Attorneys and Legal Considerations

Attorney Up! Before you get too far down the road with hiring, you need to establish good legal counsel. It's a very good idea to find an attorney with a background in employment law! I recommend a local attorney that is acquainted with Federal Law and the laws of your state. He or she should also have an idea of how those laws are likely to be interpreted in your region, county and city. Eventually you will want to invest in an experienced Human Resource professional who both knows the law and is very strengths oriented.

I hope every reader's heart is to treat every applicant and every employee with dignity and respect. To most of us these matters seem like common sense and an application of the Golden Rule. But we don't always think through these things clearly. Most of us come with pre-conceived ideas about fairness and those ideas may or may not square up with current law.

The law is not static or fixed. It's very dynamic, changing and moving. You're only going to stay on top of those changes by surrounding yourself with a good attorney and top notch Human Resource help. If you are an entrepreneur who hasn't been in business long, you may be naive about the potential risks.

While there are plenty of employers who operate on the ethical edge, there are also a few potential employees who are looking for a lawsuit and a free ride. Be careful.

Below you'll find a list of 8 Federal Guidelines that will give you a foundation to think through some core legal issues when it comes to hiring. But again, this doesn't cover state laws, which can vary widely. And it doesn't cover the specific application of state law which can vary inside a region within any given state.

Basics

The following can provide basic employment guidelines in federal law:

1- The Fourteenth Amendment to the *U.S. Constitution*
2- The Civil Rights Act of 1964
3- The Civil Rights Act of 1991
4- Supreme Court Case - *McDonnell Douglas Corp. v. Green* (1973)
5- Disparate Impact Case Law
6- Employee Selection Procedure Uniform Guidelines (1978)
7- The Americans with Disabilities Act (ADA 1990)
8- The Uniformed Services Employment and Reemployment Rights Act (USERRA 1994)

These laws, including their interpretations by individual judges and courts are the key drivers of hiring, employment testing and just about everything related to how employees and perspective employees are to be treated.

1- The Fourteenth Amendment

The *United States Constitution* is the highest law of the land. The Fourteenth Amendment of the *U.S. Constitution* requires that each and every state must guarantee equal protection for all of its citizens. Therefore, state laws must be written and enforced in a way that requires all job candidates to be given equal opportunities regardless of any category they may fall in. Today, this is generally interpreted to mean race, color, national origin, religion, gender, age or orientation although all of these categories were not included at the time. The Fourteenth Amendment also gives Congress the power to enforce equal protection of all U.S. citizens by enacting laws that support this ideal. The Civil Rights Act of 1964 and the Civil Rights Act of 1991 are two examples that build on the Fourteenth Amendment.

2- The Civil Rights Act of 1964

The Civil Rights Act of 1964 has made employment discrimination based on race, color, religion, sex or national origin illegal. Employers may legally utilize the results of any employment selection or screening assessment as long as it does not discriminate against a candidate because of race, color, national origin, religion or gender. Different Treatment and Different Impact are both prohibited under this Act of Congress. Different Treatment occurs when an employer intentionally discriminates against a candidate based on race, color, national origin, religion or gender. The core issue in different treatment cases is that employees or prospective employees from a protected group are *intentionally* treated differently from others. Different Impact occurs when an employer's process is consistently applied to all employees but that process results in a disproportionate number of individuals from protected groups in being excluded. Different Impact is illegal when the employer's hiring process is not job related or built on business necessity.

Note: The legal terminology is Disparate Treatment and Disparate Impact. I have used the term "Different" because it is more widely understood.

3- The Civil Rights Act of 1991

The Civil Rights Act of 1991 clarified several sections of the Civil Rights Act of 1964. One of the key additions found in the Civil Rights Act of 1991 is the banning of Score Adjustment based on an individual being part of a particular group. Employers are prohibited under the Civil Rights Act of 1991 from adjusting scores, using different cutoff scores, or in any way altering the scores of any test on the basis of race, color, religion, sex, or national origin.

One of the selection processes most impacted by this Act of Congress was the P.A.T. or Physical Ability Test. Due to innate physical gender differences between men and women, different physical standards were used for men and women. But this law made it clear that if men and women are taking a Physical Ability Test or assessment, they must pass using the same assessment standard for the same position or work role. This standard applies to any selection tool an employer might use. The standard for any assessment is job relatedness and business necessity. In other words the assessment must accurately measure abilities that are clearly related to the specific role an applicant is applying for. Examples of allowable evidence or demonstration include expert testimony, validation studies, statistical reports and past experience.

4- *McDonnell Douglas Corp. v. Green* (1973)

The United States Supreme Court has created an alternating burden-shifting method following the *McDonnell Douglas Corp. v. Green* (1973) case. A complainant (Someone bringing a discrimination lawsuit) may have a valid case if the following conditions are met:

1- The job candidate bringing the lawsuit is a member of a protected class based on race, color, national origin, religion, gender, age or orientation.

2- The candidate bringing the lawsuit applied and was qualified for the job.

3- The applicant or application was rejected.

If these conditions are met, the burden shifts to the employer to present evidence that there were legitimate, non-discriminatory reasons for not hiring a candidate. After the employer presents that evidence in court, the burden then shifts back to the individual bringing the lawsuit. The person bringing the lawsuit must convince the court that the employer's evidence was either false or that it was in fact, discrimination.

5- (Different) Disparate Impact Case Law:

In different impact cases, the one bringing the discrimination complaint provides evidence to prove that the hiring process or selection assessment has significant adverse impact on a protected group based on race, national origin, color, religion, gender or orientation. Statistical evidence is often used in this type of case. The burden of proof then alternates as described in the case above.

Employers have a responsibility to ensure that their selection assessments and processes do not result in discrimination. Every assessment and selection process used to make employment decisions, including both hiring and promoting, need to be carefully evaluated. That evaluation should be base on three factors:

1- Job Relatedness – Is the hiring or promotion process and assessment solidly based on abilities that are demonstrated to impact job performance?

2- Business Necessity – Is the hiring or promotion process and assessment solidly based on criteria that is necessary for the business to survive and succeed?

3- Disparate Impact – If the hiring, promotion or selection process disproportionately screens out members from a protected group based on race, national origin, color, religion, gender or orientation; then the employer needs to shift its hiring practice to something that eliminates the bias.

6- Employee Selection Procedure Uniform Guidelines (1978)

The Employee Selection Procedure Uniform Guidelines have been developed to help companies comply with the law, especially in matters of discrimination base on race, national origin, color, religion, gender or orientation. Companies are responsible for ensuring that their selection, hiring and promotion processes are in compliance with the Uniform

Guidelines. Assessments should be validated for the work roles for which they are being used.

7- The Americans with Disabilities Act (ADA 1990)

The ADA is a civil rights law that guarantees equal opportunity for qualified candidates with disabilities. It also provides enforceable standards for protection. Under this law, employers are prohibited from discriminating against "qualified individuals with disabilities." Qualified candidates are those who can perform essential functions of a work role with or without "reasonable accommodation." This is defined as "any modification or adjustment that enables an individual with a disability to participate or perform essential functions of the job". Employers are required to make reasonable accommodations for qualified individuals with what is called a "known" disability. In other words, the qualified individual who has a disability must request an adjustment or accommodation. If the request is not made, the employer is obligated to make the accommodation. The exception would be if the disability and need for the accommodation might be considered obvious. The employer and the disabled individual are to work together to identify and select a mutually acceptable and reasonable accommodation.

Companies need to ensure that selection and promotion processes and assessments test the ability of a worker to perform essential functions necessary in the position. Assessments should be given to disabled individuals in a format that does not require the use of an impaired ability, unless the ability is clearly job related. Requirements that screen out candidates with disabilities are legal only if they are assessing for job related abilities and can be considered a business necessity.

8- The Uniformed Services Employment and Reemployment Rights Act (USERRA 1994)

USERRA is the federal law that establishes rights for returning service members and responsibilities for their civilian employers. This law impacts employment, reemployment and retention in employment, when employees serve or have served in the military services. Under USERRA, an employer organization cannot discriminate against any uniformed services member in selection, reemployment, retention, promotion or any benefit of employment based on their military service.

One of the implications of USERRA on selection and assessment process is providing alternative times or make up opportunities for reemployed service people who were on military duty and as a result missed promotional testing. Unless it is impossible, organizations must provide service people a reasonable opportunity to take the same promotional test that was administered while they were deployed. When coming back, organizations must also provide the returning employees a reasonable period to prepare for any promotion examination. If the returning employee passes the test, then promotion must be made effective as of the date it would have occurred if they were not deployed.

At-Will Agreements – Don't Depend On Them

At-Will Employment Agreements are a type of employment contract common in some states. When an employee is hired "At Will", it means that the employee can be dismissed for any reason and without warning, without an employer having to establish just cause as long as the reason is not illegal. In other words, an individual still cannot be released because of race, national origin, color, religion, gender or orientation. The law is justified based on reciprocity. It's the idea that an employee can leave his or her job without reason or warning, so an employer should have the same rights. On the other hand, the law is seen as unjust by those who view the employment relationship as one based on inequality and lack of leverage or bargaining power by an employee.

My simple advice is this: Don't get sloppy when releasing an employee in a state where you have an At-Will agreement. Too many employers think that just because they are in an At-Will state they can do anything they want. Always treat departing employees with dignity and respect regardless of the reason for their release. It's the right thing to do. And it's the legally safe thing to do.

If you are a hiring manager in a corporate setting, don't assume that releasing an employee based on your superiors' request keeps you legally safe. I hired and fired in a corporate setting for eight years in multiple states. I never did anything without the best information from my Human Resource Department. In some cases I got opinions from multiple sources inside of Human Resources. Don't assume your direct superior is the most qualified person to help you with hiring and firing decisions.

If you are an entrepreneur, you probably started a business because you like to have some measure of control over who you work with. I'm all for you on that. Just don't get arrogant or sloppy with the legal part. Get good counsel and follow it closely!

Bibliography

Read This First!

1- Lou Adler, *Hire With Your Head: Using Performance-Based Hiring to Build Great Teams* (Hoboken: John Wiley and Sons, 2007).

2- Lou Adler, *Talent Rules: Using Performance-Based Hiring to Build Great Teams* (Chicago: Nightingale-Conant, 2007).

3- Jim Collins, *Good to Great – Why Some Companies Make the Leap and Others Don't* (New York: Harper Business, 2001).

4- Steve Jobs, Quote - http://smartbusinesstrends.com/insightful-hiring-quotes-lessons-9-business-experts-leaders/.

5- Tom Peters, Quote from Tom Peters Presentation Slides on Hiring, http://tompeters.com/slides/topic-presentations/.

6- Eric Schmidt & Jonathan, *How Google Works* (New York: Grand Central Publishing, 2014).

Introduction

1- Eric Schmidt & Jonathan, *How Google Works* (New York: Grand Central Publishing, 2014).

2- Jim Collins, *Good to Great – Why Some Companies Make the Leap and Others Don't* (New York: Harper Business, 2001).

3- Nicholas Lore, *The Pathfinder* (New York: Fireside/Simon and Schuster,1998), 11-13.

4- Jim Clifton, *The Coming Jobs War* (New York: Gallup Press, First Printing, 2011),106.

Chapter One - One Question That Predicts Performance

1- Marcus Buckingham and Don O. Clifton, *Now, Discover Your Strengths* (New York: Free Press/Simon and Schuster, 2001).

2- Tom Rath, *Strengthsfinder 2.0* (New York: Gallup Press, 2007).

3- Marcus Buckingham & Curt Coffman, *First, Break All The Rules* (New York: Simon & Schuster, 1999).

4- Marcus Buckingham, *The One Thing You Need to Know… About Great Managing, Great Leading, and Sustained Individual Success* (New York: Free Press, Simon & Schuster, 2005).

5- Jim Clifton, *The Coming Jobs War* (New York: Gallup Press, First Printing, 2011),106.

Chapter Two – Staffing for Passion

1- Dave Ramsey, *EntreLeadership – 20 Years of Practical Business Wisdom from the Trenches* (New York: Howard Books, Simon & Schuster, 2011).

2- Timothy Butler, *Getting Unstuck: A Guide to Discovering Your Next Career Path* (Boston: Harvard Business Press, 2007), 57.

3- Eric Schmidt & Jonathan, *How Google Works* (New York: Grand Central Publishing, 2014).

4- Mihaly Csikszentmihaly, *Flow: The Psychology of Optimal Performance* (New York: Harper Classics, 2008), 88.

5- Oprah Winfrey, *The Best of Oprah's What I Know For Sure* (New York: The Oprah Magazine, Hearst Corporation, 2000), 39.

6- Article: *Steve Jobs Hiring Top Employees*, http://www.independent.co.uk/life-style/jobs-what-look-for-steve-jobs-hiring-top-employees-a8106641.html.

7- Steve Jobs Interview, *Steve Jobs HR Philosophy, YouTube,* **https://youtu.be/rQKis2Cfpeo**.

8- Blog Post: Dan Sullivan *Strategic Coach* Batteries Included Concept, https://resources.strategiccoach.com/the-multiplier-mindset-blog/batteries-included-why-its-my-must-have-in-a-team-member.

9- Cliff Freeman Agency, *Stapes Price Guy Commercial,* http://www.tvspots.tv/video/8862/staples--price-guy.

10- Nathan Gebhard, Brian McAllister and Mike Marriner with Jay Sacher, Alyssa Frank, Annie Mais, Jaime Zehler and Willie Witte, *Roadmap* (San Francisco: Chronicle Books, San Francisco, 2015), 156-157.

11- Ed Catmull, *Creativity, Inc. – Overcoming The Unseen Forces That Stand In The Way Of True Inspiration* (New York: Random House, 2014), 8-20.

12- Janet Attwood, Interview with Lilou Mace, *YouTube*, October 28, 2013, Accessed May 3, 2016, https://youtu.be/78NGfghtyTo .

Chapter Three – Staffing for Talent

1- Lady Gaga and Jeppe Laursen , Song Lyrics: *Baby You Were Born This Way* (Santa Monica: Streamline Records, 2011).

2- Don O. Clifton and Paula Nelson, *Soar With Your Strengths* (New York: Dell Publishing,1992).

3- Liz Wiseman, *Multipliers: How The Best Leaders Make Everyone Smarter* (New York: Harper Collins, 2010).

4- Marcus Buckingham and Don O. Clifton, *Now, Discover Your Strengths* (New York: Free Press/Simon and Schuster, 2001).

5- Scott Adams, *Dilbert* Creator, *"The Knack"* from *Dilbert: The Complete Series* (DVD) (Culver City: Sony Pictures, 2000), Season 1 - Episode 9.

6- Howard Gardner, *Multiple Intelligences* (New York: Basic Books, New York, 1993), 17-26.

7-Margaret E. Broadley, *Your Natural Gifts* (McLean, Virginia: EPM Publications, 1977), 3-7.

8- *O*NET (The Occupational Information Network),* website: https://www.onetonline.org/find/descriptor/browse/Abilities/.

9- Tom Rath & Barry Conchie, *Strengths Based Leadership* (New York: Gallup Press, 2008), 24.

10- Marcus Buckingham & Curt Coffman, *First, Break All The Rules* (New York: Simon & Schuster, 1999).

11- Lori Goler, VP of People, *Facebook*, Interview with *Business Insider,* http://www.businessinsider.com/facebook-interview-question-2017-2.

Chapter Four – Staffing for Personality

1- Kate Ward, *Personality Style at Work: The Secret to Working With Almost Anyone* (New York: McGraw Hill, 2012), 5.

2- Richard Branson, founder of *Virgin*, Interview with *LinkedIn,* https://business.linkedin.com/talent-solutions/blog/recruiting-tips/2016/7-hiring-rules-that-have-lead-sir-richard-branson-to-success.

3- Colin Powell, *It Worked For Me* (New York: Harper Collins, 2012), 95-96.

Chapter Five – Staffing for Values

1- Nathan Gebhard, Brian McAllister and Mike Marriner with Jay Sacher, Alyssa Frank, Annie Mais, Jaime Zehler and Willie Witte, *Roadmap* (San Francisco: Chronicle Books, San Francisco, 2015), 171-172.

2- Eduard Spranger*, Types of Men: the Psychology and Ethics of Personality* (Halle, Germany: M. Niemeyer,1928).

Chapter Six – Staffing for Knowledge

1- *O*NET (The Occupational Information Network),* website: https://www.onetonline.org/find/descriptor/browse/Knowledge/.

2- Thomas Edison, *General Knowledge Hiring Questionnaire,* http://www.openculture.com/2015/03/thomas-edisons-146-question-knowledge-test-for-prospective-employees.html.

Chapter Seven – Staffing for Skills

1- Jay Niblick, *What's Your Genius?* (St. James Books, 2009), 26.

2- Jim Barrett & Kogan Page*, Ultimate Aptitude Tests* (London: Kogan-Page, 2012), 4.

3- O*NET (The Occupational Information Network), website: https://www.onetonline.org/find/descriptor/browse/Skills/

4- Deborah Koehn Lloyd, *Your Vocational Credo* (Downers Grove: InterVarsity Press, 2015), 75-76.

Chapter Eight – Staffing for Character

1- Robert K. Cooper, *Executive EQ: Emotional Intelligence in Leadership and Organizations* (New York: Perigee, 1997), 166-167.

2- *The Google Code of Conduct – Don't Be Evil,* https://abc.xyz/investor/other/google-code-of-conduct.html.

3- Stephen M.R. Covey with Rebecca Merrill, *The Speed of Trust* (New York: Free Press/Simon and Schuster, 2001).

4- Jim Loehr, *The Only Way To Win: How Building Character Drives Higher Achievement and Greater Fulfillment in Business and Life* (New York: Hyperion, 2012).

Chapter Nine – Selecting for Other Dimensions

1- Bobb Biehl, *Team Profile*, formerly *Role Preference Inventory* (Mount Dora: Masterplanning Group).

2- Nassim Nicholas Taleb, *Antifragile: Things That Gain From Disorder* (New York: Random House, 2014).

3- Michael Breus, *The Power of When* (New York: Little Brown, 2016).

4- Eric Weiner, *The Geography of Genius* (New York: Simon and Schuster, 2016).

5- James Marcus Bach, *Secrets of a Buccaneer-Scholar (*New York: Scribner/Simon and Schuster, 2009), 5.

6- Lazlo Block, *Work Rules!* (New York: Twelve, Hachette Book Group, 2015), 66.

7- Jim Cathcart, *The Acorn Principle* (New York: St. Martins Press,1999).

8- Debra Angel MacDougall and Elisabeth Harney Sanders-Park, *The 6 Reasons You'll Get the Job* (New York: Prentice Hall Press, 2010).

Chapter Ten – Convergence: Selecting for Integration

1- Eric Schmidt & Jonathan, *How Google Works* (New York: Grand Central Publishing, 2014).

2- Timothy Butler, *Getting Unstuck: A Guide to Discovering Your Next Career Path* (Boston: Harvard Business Press, 2007), 57.

3- Anne Linden with Kathrin Perutz*, Mindworks* (Kansas City: Andrews McMeel, 1997), 205.

4- Mihaly Csikszentmihaly, *Flow: The Psychology of Optimal Performance* (New York: Harper Classics, 2008), 88.

5- *Harrison Assessments,* http://www.trustedcoach.com/wp-content/uploads/2015/01/HATS-175_Trait_Descriptions.pdf.

Chapter Eleven – "A" Positions: Identify Mission Critical Roles

1- Logan Loomis, *Getting the People Equation Right: How to Get the Right People in the Right Jobs and Keep Them* (Baton Rouge: L. Loomis, 2010).

2- Ray Dalio, *Principles* (New York: Simon and Schuster, 2017).

3- Marshall Goldsmith, *Triggers: Creating Behavior that Lasts* (New York: Crown Business, 2015), 62,141.

Chapter Twelve – The "A" Candidate Profile

1- Sally Bibb, *Strengths-Based Recruitment & Development: A practical guide to transforming management strategy for business results* (London: Kogan Page, 2016).

2- Jim Benson, Tonianne DeMaria Barry, *Personal Kanban: Mapping Work | Navigating Life* (Seattle: Modus Operandi Press, 2009).

3- Timothy Butler, *Getting Unstuck: A Guide to Discovering Your Next Career Path* (Boston: Harvard Business Press, 2007).

4- *O*NET (The Occupational Information Network),* Accountant Summary: https://www.onetonline.org/link/summary/13-2011.01.

Chapter Thirteen – Attraction Advertising

1- *O*NET (The Occupational Information Network),* Accountant Summary: https://www.onetonline.org/link/summary/13-2011.01.

2- Roy H. Williams, *Secret Formulas of the Wizard of Ads* (Austin: Bard Press, 1999), 168-169.

3- Lazlo Block, *Work Rules!* (New York: Twelve, Hachette Book Group, 2015), 83.

Chapter Fifteen – Application

1- Application Acknowledgement Letter from The Marcus Buckingham Company.

2- Jacob Ganz, *The Truth About Van Halen And Those Brown M&Ms* (National Public Radio), https://www.npr.org/sections/therecord/2012/02/14/146880432/the-truth-about-van-halen-and-those-brown-m-ms.

Chapter Sixteen - Assessments

1- Tony Robbins, *Inc. Magazine interview*, https://www.inc.com/magazine/201610/how-tony-robbins-hires-employees.html.

2- Ray Dalio, *Principles* (New York: Simon and Schuster, 2017).

3- Keith Coaley, *An Introduction to Psychological Assessment and Psychometrics* (London: Sage, 2010), 7.

4- Frank Parsons, *Choosing a Vocation* (New York: Houghton Mifflin, 1909).

Chapter Seventeen – Audition: Strengths Oriented Interviewing

1- Joel Spolsky, *Smart and Gets Things Done* (New York: Apress, 2012), 68, 83.

2- Miranda Kalinowski, Global Head of Recruiting, *Facebook*, Interview with *Business Insider,* http://www.businessinsider.com/facebook-interview-question-2017-2.

3- Lazlo Block, *Wired* Magazine Interview, https://www.wired.com/2015/04/hire-like-google/.

4- Frank Schmidt and John Hunter, *The Validity and Utility of Selection Methods in Personnel Psychology: Practical and Theoretical Implications of 85 Years of Research Findings,* http://citeseerx.ist.psu.edu/viewdoc/download?doi=10.1.1.172.1733&rep=rep1&type=pdf.

5- Tony Robbins, *Inc. Magazine interview*, https://www.inc.com/magazine/201610/how-tony-robbins-hires-employees.html.

6- Crockett Johnson, *Harold and the Purple Crayon* (New York: Harper Collins, 1955).

7- Deborah Koehn Lloyd, *Your Vocational Credo – Practical Steps to Discover Your Unique Purpose* (Downers Grove: InterVarsity Press, 2015)

8- Adam Bryant, *3 Completely Random Interview Questions That Are Actually Insightful, YouTube,*
https://www.inc.com/video/adam-bryant/3-key-questions-you-must-ask-every-new-hire.html.

Chapter Eighteen – Appointments: Making The Selection

1- Kip Tindell, *Uncontainable: How Passion, Commitment, and Conscious Capitalism Built a Business Where Everyone Thrives* (New York: Hachette Book Group, 2014), 53.

2- Eric Schmidt & Jonathan, *How Google Works* (New York: Grand Central Publishing, 2014), 122-124.

Chapter Nineteen – Autopsy Your Process

1- John Maxwell, Article:
 http://www.johnmaxwell.com/blog/understanding-underperformance.

2- Kobe Bryant, Interview:
https://youtu.be/D__9I-dTQMw

Chapter Twenty – *Agile* Hiring

1- Hirotaka Takeuchi and Ikujiro Nonaka, *The New New Product Development Game (*Boston: Harvard Business Review, January 1986), https://hbr.org/1986/01/the-new-new-product-development-game.

2- Tycho Press, *Scrum Basics: A Very Quick Guide to Agile Project Management* (Berkeley: Tycho Press, 2015).

3- Jeff Sutherland, *Scrum: The Art of Doing Twice the Work in Half the Time* (New York: Crown Business, 2014).

4- Tridibesh Satpathy - Lead Author, *Scrum Study: A Guide to the Scrum Body of Knowledge* (Phoenix: Scrumstudy, 2013).

5- *"Write the vision and make it plain on tablets, that he may run who reads it."* This passage from Habakkuk 2:2 is taken from the New King James Version published by Thomas Nelson.

6- Jim Benson, Tonianne DeMaria Barry, *Personal Kanban: Mapping Work Navigating Life* (Seattle: Modus Operandi Press, 2009).

7- Daniel Markovitz, *A Factory of One: Applying Lean Principles to Banish Waste and Improve Personal Performance* (Boca Raton: CRC Press, 2012).

Chapter Twenty One – Attorneys & Legal Considerations

1- The Fourteenth Amendment to the *U.S. Constitution*
https://www.law.cornell.edu/wex/employment_discrimination.

2- The Civil Rights Act of 1964,
https://www.eeoc.gov/laws/statutes/titlevii.cfm.

3- The Civil Rights Act of 1991,
https://www.eeoc.gov/eeoc/history/35th/1990s/civilrights.html.

4- Supreme Court Case - *McDonnell Douglas Corp. v. Green* (1973),
https://www.eeoc.gov/eeoc/history/35th/thelaw/supreme_court.html.

5- Disparate Impact Case Law,
https://www.eeoc.gov/eeoc/history/35th/1965-71/shaping.html.

6- Employee Selection Procedure Uniform Guidelines (1978),
http://www.uniformguidelines.com.

7- The Americans with Disabilities Act (ADA 1990),
https://www.eeoc.gov/eeoc/publications/fs-ada.cfm.

8- The Uniformed Services Employment and Reemployment Rights Act
(USERRA 1994),
https://www1.eeoc.gov//eeoc/newsroom/release/2-28-
12.cfm?renderforprint=1.

9- Industrial/Organizational Solutions – Laws Related To Employment
Testing and Practices,
https://iosolutions.com/wp-content/uploads/2017/09/Laws-Related-to-
Employment-Testing-and-Practices-2017.pdf.

Further Reading

To write this book, I've stood on a lot of other people's shoulders. I am approaching 2000 books in my human potential and career development library. A few hundred are relevant to Strengths Oriented Staffing. Listed below are around 100 of the best references I own and recommend for their wisdom in the steps and categories used in this book. A single book can never include everything you need to know. If you are building a career, it would be valuable to start your own library. Many of these resources will add depth to what I've said on the subject. If you work anywhere as a hiring manager or human resource professional, you are cheating your candidates and associates by not acquainting yourself with the thinking, strategies and experiences of other experts in the field. The resources below are a good start!

Strengths Based Selection and Hiring

The Strong Manager Program, The Marcus Buckingham Company
Getting the People Equation Right: How to Get the Right People in the Right Jobs and Keep Them, Logan Loomis
Handbook of Human Abilities: Definitions, Measurements and Job Task Responsibilities, Edwin A. Fleishman and Maureen E. Reilly
*An Occupational Information System For The 21st Century: The Development of O*NET*, Edited by Norman G. Peterson, Michael D. Mumford, Walter C. Borman, P. Richard Jeanneret and Edwin Fleishman
Aptitude Testing, Clark Hull
Strengths-Based Recruitment and Development: A Practical Guide to Transforming Talent Management Strategy for Business Results, Sally Bibb
Essentials of Personnel Assessment & Selection, Scott Highhouse, Dennis Doverspike and Robert M. Guion
Assessing Personality, Robert R. Holt
An Introduction to Psychological Assessment and Psychometrics, Keith Coaley
Talent Rules, Lou Adler
The Talent Solution, Edward L. Gubman
Build An A Team: Play to Their Strengths and Lead Them Up the Learning Curve, Whitney Johnson
Work Rules! Insights From Inside Google, Laslo Bock
How Google Works, Eric Schmidt & Jonathan Rosenberg

Strengths and Business Leadership

The Effective Executive, Peter Drucker
Managing Oneself, Peter Drucker
Organizing Genius, Warren Bennis
Talent, Tom Peters
Good To Great, Jim Collins
Winning, Jack and Suzy Welch
Multipliers: How The Best Leaders Make Everyone Smarter, Liz Wiseman
The Ten Faces of Innovation, Tom Kelly
Shine, Edward Hallowell
Working Together: Why Great Partnerships Succeed, Michael Eisner with Aaron Cohen
Team Genius: The New Science of High-Performing Teams, Rich Karlgaard and Michael S. Malone
Surrounded by Geniuses: Unlocking the Brilliance in Yourself, Your Colleagues and Your Organization, Dr. Alan S. Gregerman
Collaborative Intelligence: Thinking with People Who Think Differently, Dawna Markova, Ph.D. and Angie McArthur
Powers Of Two: Finding the Essence of Innovation in Creative Pairs, Joshua Wolf Shenk
Leading Apple with Steve Jobs: Management Lessons from a Controversial Genius, Jay Elliot
Inside Apple: How America's Most Admired and Secretive Company Really Works, Adam Lashinsky

Gallup/Marcus Buckingham Family

Soar With Your Strengths, Don O. Clifton and Paula Nelson
Now, Discover Your Strengths, Marcus Buckingham and Donald Clifton
Strengths Finder 2.0, Tom Rath
StandOut 2.0, Marcus Buckingham
Go, Put Your Strengths To Work, Marcus Buckingham
The Truth About You, Marcus Buckingham
DVD- Trombone Player Wanted, Marcus Buckingham
Find Your Strongest Life, Marcus Buckingham
The One Thing You Need To Know, Marcus Buckingham
First Break All The Rules, Marcus Buckingham and Curt Coffman
Strengths Based Leadership, Tom Rath and Barrie Conchie
Follow This Path: How the World's Greatest Organizations Drive Growth by Unleashing Human Potential, Curt Coffman and Gabriel Gonzalez-Molina, Ph.D.
Human Sigma: Managing The Employee-Customer Encounter, John H. Fleming and Jim Asplund
Animals Inc., Kenneth A. Tucker
Strengths Based Selling, Tony Rutigliano, Brian Brim
Discover Your Sales Strengths, Tony Rutigliano, Benson Smith

Teach With Your Strengths, Rosanne Liesveld, Jo Ann Miller with Jennifer Robison

Are You Fully Charged?, Tom Rath

Entrepreneurial Strengthsfinder, Jim Clifton and Sangeeta Bharadwaj Badal, Ph.D.

The Coming Jobs War, Jim Clifton

The Power of 2: How to Make the Most of Your Partnerships at Work and in Life, Rodd Wagner and Gale Muller

STRENGTHSQUEST: Discover and Develop Your Strengths In Academics, Career, and Beyond, Donald O. Clifton, Ph.D. & Edward "Chip" Anderson, Ph.D.

12 Elements of Great Managing, Rodd Wagner & James K. Harter, Ph.D.

Johnson O'Connor/The Highlands Family

Don't Waste Your Talent, Bob McDonald and Don E. Hutcheson

Hardwired: Taking the Road to Delphi and Uncovering Your Talents, Dr. Tom Tavantzis with Paul Jablow

Understanding Your Aptitudes, Johnson O'Connor Research Foundation

Your Natural Gifts, Margaret Broadley

Learning To Use Your Aptitudes, Dean Trembly

Know Your Real Abilities, Charles V. and Magaret E. Broadley

Structural Visualization, Johnson O'Connor

Ideaphoria, Johnson O'Connor

Unsolved Business Problems, Johnson O'Connor

Square Pegs In Square Holes, Margaret E. Broadley

The Unique Individual, Johnson O'Connor

Be Yourself: Analyzing Your Innate Aptitudes, Margaret E. Broadley

The Too Many Aptitude Woman, Johnson O'Connor

The Aptitude Handbook: A Guide to the AIMS Program, *Aptitude Inventory Measurement Service*

Job Search/Career Services Family

Why You Can't Be Anything You Want to Be, Arthur Miller Jr. with William Hendricks

Getting Unstuck: A Guide to Discovering Your Next Career Path, Timothy Butler

Choosing a Vocation, Frank Parsons, Ph.D.

Making Vocational Choices: A Theory of Careers, John L. Holland

Business Model You: The One-Page Method for Reinventing Your Career, Tim Clark, Alexander Osterwalder and Yves Pigneur

Career Satisfaction and Success, Bernard Haldane

How to Make a Habit of Success, Bernard Haldane

Franklin Covey

The 8th Habit, Stephen Covey
Great Work, Great Career, Stephen Covey and Jennifer Colosimo

U.K. Families

The Strengths Book, Alex Linley, Janet Willars, Robert Biswas-Diener
Average to A+, Alex Linley
The Strengths Way, Mike Pegg
The Strengths Toolbox, Mike Pegg

D.I.S.C – 4 Quadrant Personality Style Families

Self Awareness: The Hidden Driver of Success and Satisfaction, Travis Bradbury
The Platinum Rule: Discover The Four Basic Business Personalities and How They Can Lead You To Success, Tony Alessandra, Ph.D., and Michael J. O'Connor, Ph.D.
Leading From Your Strengths, John Trent and Rodney Cox
The Essential DISC Training Workbook, Jason Hedge
Who Do You Think You Are…Anyway?, Robert A. Rohm, Ph.D. and E. Chris Carey
Positive Personality Profiles, Robert A. Rohm, Ph.D.
Personality Style at Work: The Secret to Working With Almost Anyone, Kate Ward
The 8 Dimensions of Leadership, Jeffrey Sugerman, Mark Scullard, Emma Wilhelm
Color Your Future, Dr. Taylor Hartman, Ph.D.
The People Code, Dr. Taylor Hartman, Ph.D.
True Colors, Roger Birkman, Ph.D.
Top Brain, Bottom Brain: Surprising Insights Into How You Think, Stephen M. Kosslyn, Ph.D., and G. Wayne Miller
Winning From Within: A Breakthrough Method For Leading, Living, and Lasting Change, Erica Ariel Fox
Social Style Management: Developing Productive Work Relationships, Robert Bolton and Dorothy Grover Bolton
The Four Elements of Success, Laurie Beth Jones

The Kolbe Family

Powered by Instinct, Kathy Kolbe
The Conative Connection, Kathy Kolbe
Pure Instinct, Kathy Kolbe

The Strategic Coach Family

Unique Ability, Catherine Nomura and Julia Waller with Shannon Waller

Unique Ability 2.0, Catherine Nomura and Julia Waller with Shannon Waller
Unique Ability 2.0 Discovery, Catherine Nomura and Julia Waller with Shannon Waller
Pure Genius CDs, Dan Sullivan

Miscellaneous Families

Where We Belong: Journeys That Show Us The Way, Hoda Kotb with Jane Lorenzini
What's Your Genius?, Jay Niblick
Quiet: The Power of Introverts in a World That Can't Stop Talking, Susan Cain
Me, Myself, And Us: The Science of Personality and the Art of Well-Being, Brian R. Little
The Acorn Principle, Jim Cathcart
What You're Really Meant To Do, Robert Steven Kaplan
One Big Thing, Phil Cooke
Practical Genius, Gina Amaro Rudan
Succeed On Your Own Terms, Hank Greenberg and Patrick Sweeney
Liberating Everyday Genius, Mary-Elaine Jacobsen

Myers-Briggs Family

www.type-Coach.com
www.myersbriggs.org
Gifts Differing, Isabel Briggs Myers with Peter B. Myers
Katherine and Isabel, Frances Wright Saunders
Personality Type: An Owner's Manual, Lenore Thomson
Portraits of Temperament, David Keirsey
Please Understand Me, David Keirsey and Marilyn Bates
Do What You Are, Paul D. Tieger & Barbara Barron-Tieger
Type Talk at Work: How the 16 Personality Types Determine Your Success on the Job, Otto Kroeger with Janet M. Thuesen and Hile Rutledge
Multiple Intelligences & Personality Type, Dario Nardi

The Enneagram Family

The Enneagram, Helen Palmer
Bringing Out The Best In Yourself At Work, Ginger Lapid-Bogda, Ph.D.

Job Crafting Family

Article - What Is Job Crafting and Why Does It Matter?, Justin M. Berg, Amy Wrzesniewski and Jane Dutton
Job Crafting Exercise, Justin M. Berg, Amy Wrzesniewski and Jane Dutton

Article - Hate Your Job? Here's How To Re-Shape It!, Jeremy Caplan
Mind Tools – Shaping Your Job To Fit You Better, The Mind Tools Website

Strengths in Education

Creative Schools, Ken Robinson, Ph.D. and Lou Aronica
The Element, Ken Robinson
Finding Your Element, Ken Robinson
Shop Class As Soulcraft, Matthew B. Crawford
The Math Myth And Other STEM Delusions, Andrew Hacker
7 Kinds of Smart, Thomas Armstrong

Strengths Development

Talent Is Never Enough, John C. Maxwell
How Successful People Grow, John C. Maxwell
The Slight Edge, Jeff Olson
The Compound Effect: Jumpstart Your Income, Your Life, Your Success, Darren Hardy
Mastery, George Leonard
Secrets of a Buccaneer Scholar: How Self Education and the Pursuit of Passion Can Lead to a Lifetime of Success, James Marcus Bach
Learning As A Way Of Being: Strategies for Survival in a World of Permanent White Water, Peter B. Vaill
Mindset: The New Psychology of Success, Carol S. Dweck, Ph.D.

Success Movement Books

The Success Principles, Jack Canfield
See You At The Top, Zig Ziglar
Lead the Field, Earl Nightingale
Unlimited Power, Anthony Robbins
Awaken The Giant Within, Anthony Robbins
Notes From A Friend, Anthony Robbins
8 To Be Great, Richard St. John
Move Ahead With Possibility Thinking, Dr. Robert Schuller
The Psychology of Winning, Dr. Denis Waitley
The Winners Edge, Dr. Denis Waitley
University of Success, Og Mandino

Strengths Based Goal Setting

The Right Mountain, Jim Hayhurst, Sr.
Stop Setting Goals... If You'd Rather Solve Problems, Bobb Biehl
Article - Follow Your River, by Earl Nightingale

Strengths Based Parables

Animals Inc., Kenneth A. Tucker
Kingdomality: An Ingenious New Way to Triumph in Management,
Sheldon Bowles, Richard Silvano & Susan Silvano
The Angel Inside, Chris Widener

NLP (Neuro-Linguistic Programing) "Meta Programs" and "Parts"

Figuring Out People, Bob G. Bodenhamer and L. Michael Hall
Wired for Success, Wendy Jago
Mindworks, Anne Linden

Sports Strengths

The Sports Gene, David Epstein
Cracking the Code: The Winning Ryder Cup Strategy-Making It Work for You, Paul Azinger and Dr. Ron Braund
Your Key to Sports Success, Jon P. Niednagel
Brain Types, Jon P. Niednagel
Brain Types Audio Program & Workbook, Jon P. Niednagel
The Perfect Team, Multiple Writers
Sybervision: Muscle Memory Programming for Every Sport, Steven DeVore and Gregory R. Devore with Mike Michaelson

Disabilities as Strengths in Disguise, Neurodiversity

The Power of Neurodiversity, Thomas Armstrong
The Autistic Brain: Thinking Across The Spectrum, Temple Grandin and Richard Panek
Article-The Dyslexic CEO: Charles Schwab, Richard Branson, Craig McCaw, & John Chambers triumphed over America's No. 1 Learning Disorder and Your Kids Can Too, Betsy Morris in Fortune Magazine, May 2002
The Gift of Dyslexia: Why Some of the Smartest People Can't Read... and How They Can Learn, Ronald D. Davis with Eldon M. Braun
Be Different: Adventures of a Free-Range Aspergian, John Elder Robinson
The Gift of ADHD, Lara Honos-Webb
Asperger's from the Inside Out, Michael John Carley
Developing Talents: Careers for Individuals with Asperger's Syndrome and High Functioning Autism, Temple Grandin, Kate Duffy, Tony Attwood
How to Find Work That Works for People with Asperger Syndrome: The Ultimate Guide for Getting People With Asperger Syndrome into the Workplace (and Keeping Them There!), Gail Hawkins

Passion/Dream Job Family

The Dream Manager, Matthew Kelly

Teamworks, Barbara Sher & Annie Gottlieb
The Passion Test: The Effortless path to Discovering Your Destiny,
Janet Bray Attwood and Chris Attwood

The Faith Family

Fulfill Your Life, Ken Van Wyk
Living Your Strengths, Albert L. Winseman, Donald O. Clifton and Curt
Liesveld
Cure for the Common Life, Max Lucado
Instinct: The Power to Unleash Your Inborn Drive, T.D. Jakes
Destiny: Step Into Your Purpose, T.D. Jakes
S.H.A.P.E.: Finding and Fulfilling Your Unique Purpose For Life, Eric
Rees
You've Got Style DVD, Andy Stanley and North Point Community Church
What You Do Best In The Body of Christ, Bruce Bugbee and Willow
Creek Community Church
Soul Print: Discovering Your Divine Destiny, Mark Batterson and
National Community Church
Destiny Finder, Michael Brodeur
What's Your God Language?, Dr. Myra Perrine
The Three Colors of Ministry, Christian A. Schwarz
Discovering Your Ministry Identity, Paul R. Ford
Your Spiritual Gift Can Help Your Church Grow, Peter C. Wagner
Why Your Calling Is Critical CD, Tony Evans
Extraordinary, John Bevere
Soulprint, Mark Batterson
The Cause Within You, Matthew Barnett
For This I Was Born, Brian Houston
Recognizing Your Potential, Dr. Myles Munroe
Releasing Your Potential, Dr. Myles Munroe
Maximizing Your Potential, Dr. Myles Munroe
Discover Who You Are, Jane A.G. Kise, David Stark, Sandra Krebs Hirsh
Developing Your S.H.A.P.E. To Serve Others DVD, Featuring Bruce
Wilkinson, Joe Stowell, and Carol Kent
Wired That Way, Marita Littauer and Florence Littauer
Wired That Way DVD, Marita Littauer and Florence Littauer
The Law of Recognition, Mike Murdock
Get A Life, Reggie McNeal
How to Deal with Annoying People, Bob Phillips and Kimberly Alyn
Releasing Spiritual Gifts Today, Jim W. Goll
The Seer, Jim W. Goll
School Of The Prophets, Kris Vallotton
The Gift In You, Dr. Caroline Leaf
Switch On Your Brain, Dr. Caroline Leaf

Dollars - Making Your Strengths Pay

The Art of Money Getting, P.T. Barnum

The Millionaire Next Door, Thomas J. Stanley and William D. Danko
The Millionaire Mind, Thomas J. Stanley and William D. Danko
Obliquity, John Kay
Purple Cow, Seth Godin
Linchpin, Seth Godin
Getting Everything You Can Out Of All You've Got, Jay Abraham
Your Secret Wealth, Jay Abraham
Differentiate or Die, Jack Trout
Positioning: The Battle for Your Mind, Ries and Trout
Compete, Byron Reeves and J. Leighton Read
Hidden Marketing Assets, Richard Johnson

The Science Behind Strengths

Frames of Mind: The Theory of Multiple Intelligences, Howard Gardner
Multiple Intelligences, Howard Gardner
The Sports Gene, David Epstein
The Blank Slate: The Modern Denial of Human Nature, Steven Pinker
Born That Way: Genes | Behavior | Personality, William Wright
You Are Extraordinary, Roger J. Williams
The Biology of Success, Dr. Bob Arnot

More Books by Dale Cobb

The STRENGTHSPATH Principle: Your Roadmap to Career Success

The STRENGTHSPATH Time Manager

Dream Job!!! A Strengths Based Guide To Job Search

Take This Job and Shape It!

Look for these coming titles in the SUCCESSPATH Series:

The STRENGTHSPATH Guide to Selection and Hiring

The SUCCESSPATH Strategies: A Guide To Universal Success Principles

The STRENGTHSPATH Strategies: Succeeding by Doing What You Do Best

Crazy Good: A STRENGTHSPATH Guide to Discovering Your Natural Talents

Insanely Great: A STRENGTHSPATH Guide to Developing Your Talents Into Strengths

Wildly Successful: A STRENGTHSPATH Guide to Delivering Your Strengths in the Workplace

The STRENGTHSPATH Manager & Leader

The STRENGTHSPATH Sales Person

The STRENGTHSPATH Parent

Maximize Your Ministry: A STRENGTHSPATH Guide to Doing What You Do Best

The STRENGTHSPATH Educator

The Daily STRENGTHSPATH

SUCCESSPATH Sprint Coaching

One-to-One Sprints ☆ 60-Minute Seminars ☆ Workshops

Modeling Projects ☆ Performance Research

Strengths Assessments ☆ Selection ☆ Outplacement

Strengths Oriented Career Development Sprints
Arrive! - Strengths Oriented Goal Sprints
Strengths Oriented Time Management Sprints
"A-Game" Sprints
Service Oriented Selling Sprints
Storyboarding – Customer Experience Journey Sprints

Connect Online

Follow Our SUCCESSPATH Sixty Second Seminars

LinkedIn https://www.linkedin.com/in/dalecobb

Facebook
https://www.facebook.com/successpathcareerdevelopment/

Twitter https://twitter.com/strengthspath

Website http://www.successpathcareerdevelopment.com

Vimeo https://vimeo.com/dalecobb

YouTube https://www.youtube.com/user/daleacobb

Tumblr https://www.tumblr.com/blog/dalecobb

Contact

Dale Cobb
P.O. Box 870
Grover Beach, CA 93483
805.668.9600

www.ingramcontent.com/pod-product-compliance
Lightning Source LLC
Chambersburg PA
CBHW071258220526
45468CB00001B/180